Magazine
Design

Edited by
Chris Foges

Magazine
Design

RotoVision

A RotoVision Book
Published and Distributed
by RotoVision SA
Rue Du Bugnon 7
1299 Crans-Près-Céligny
Switzerland

RotoVision SA
Sales and Production Office
Sheridan House
112-116a Western Road
Hove, East Sussex
BN3 1DD, UK
Tel: +44 (0)1273 72 72 68
Fax: +44 (0)1273 72 72 69
e-mail: sales@RotoVision.com

Distributed to the trade
in the United States by
Watson-Guptill Publications
1515 Broadway
New York, NY 10036

ISBN 2-88046-450-1

Book designed by Struktur Design
Photography by Xavier Young

Production and separations
by ProVision Pte. Ltd. in SIngapore
Tel: +65 334 7720
Fax: +65 334 7721

Contents

06		Introduction
12	Packaging	
14		Interview
		with David Hillman
18		Front covers
20		Mastheads
24		Cover lines
25		Bar-codes, dates and prices
26		Cover images
28		Cover styles
30		Cover sets
36		Guest designers
38		Spines
39		Back covers
42		Binding
44		Bellybands
46		Boxes and bags
48	Format	
50		Interview
		with Fernando Gutiérrez
54		Little/large
60	Navigation	
62		Interview
		with Simon Esterson
66		Contents pages
72		Credits
74		Editorials
76		Navigation techniques
80		Dividers
82		Section changes
86		Standfirsts
88	Structure	
90		Interview
		with Mark Porter
94		Pagination and advertising
98		Typography
106		Captions
108	Images	
110		Interview
		with Stephen Gan
114		Picture treatment
122		Illustration
126	Systems	
128		Interview
		with Vince Frost
132		Information systems
138	Webzines	
140		Interview
		with Roger Black
144		Similarities and differences
150		Dual versions
152		The future
156		Contact details
157		Further reading
158		Credits/acknowledgements

Neue Graphik
Issue: 17, 18, 1965
Art directors:
Richard P. Lohse
J. Müller-Brockmann
Hans Neuberg
Carlo L. Vivarelli
Switzerland

·roduction

Since mass literacy coincided with technological leaps forward in the mid-19th century, magazines have played a significant part in the daily lives of people in almost every sector of society: they cater for every profession, interest, hobby and whim. After a century of growing popularity, many predicted that television would kill the magazine along with the newspaper; instead, magazines adapted, and the number published today greatly exceeds that in production at the advent of television. Today, 150 million people across the globe turn to the World Wide Web for information and entertainment, and again, magazines have adapted: hundreds now exist either in print and on-line versions, or solely in digital form. Even among those that exist solely in print form, elements of style have been borrowed from the new media to make the magazine more contemporary. If the market for printed magazines disappears completely by the time this book is published, large parts – though by no means all of it – will become irrelevant. I do not think this is likely, however. Magazines have a special place in popular culture and in the affections of their readers. Magazines may have to adapt even further to maintain their uniqueness and value, but that is what writers, editors and magazine designers have been doing for 150 years: take almost any popular magazine from any era, and what you have is the best possible record of contemporary aesthetics, concerns and attitudes – it's what makes magazines so interesting.

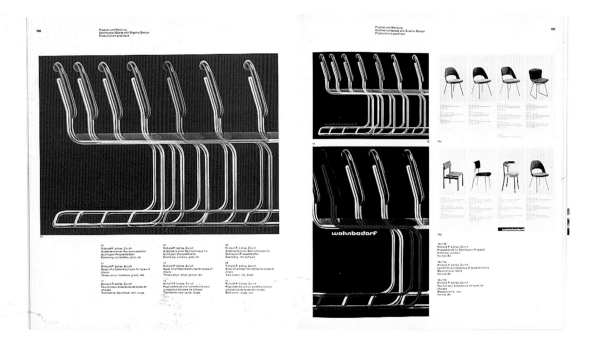

National Geographic
Issue: Apr 1958
Illustrations editor:
Herbert S. Wilburn Jr.
USA

National Geographic
Issue: Feb 1997
Layout and
design editor:
Constance H. Phelps
USA

What is a magazine?

Stand in front of a magazine rack anywhere in the world, and before you sits a dazzling array – hundreds of front covers competing for attention, each redolent with promise of what lies within. Many bear household names: *Vogue*, *GQ*, *Sports Illustrated*, *Playboy*, *National Geographic*, *Time*, *Newsweek*, *Life*, *The Economist*. These international brands are what come into the heads of most people when they think of magazines. And such consumer monthlies and news weeklies are the most visible, best known members of the periodical world. But beyond those, often away from the magazine rack, a plethora of lesser-known titles perform subtly different tasks: trade titles, newspaper supplements, customer magazines, fanzines and, today, webzines, exist in their thousands, catering for readers with specific interests, both personal and professional. Anywhere you have a group of people interested in a topic, and an individual or organisation with enough motivation to communicate with them, you'll find a magazine to bridge the gap.

The word magazine is borrowed from Arabic, in which it means 'storehouse'; The magazines we read are essentially a collection of diverse elements – articles and photographs – yoked together by a common feature. *Accountancy Age*, for example, is a storehouse of pieces of information about various aspects of accountancy, assembled by an editor, and appealing to those with a specific interest in that subject. In that context, the designer's job is two-fold: first, the design must give expression and personality to those diverse elements, so that they might be recognised as a coherent whole, attracting the reader in the first instance and then building brand loyalty. Second, the elements must be arranged in such a way that the reader can find within the 'storehouse' the individual items in which they are interested.

Who produces magazines?

Just as magazines are composed of a number of diverse, yet similar elements, so they are compiled by a variety of people, whose jobs, though distinct and different from one another, overlap in areas. While most magazines are collaborative efforts, they are also hierarchical environments where great significance is attached to job titles: editor, sub-editor, assistant editor, deputy editor, features editor, contributing editor, editor-at-large, editorial director – the permutations are almost endless, and almost endlessly significant to those involved. The status attributed to a particular job title, and the responsibilities that go with it vary from publication to publication. In some publishing houses, a decision on which cover image to use, for example, will be left entirely up to the art director. In others, the editor will want to give their opinion as well. In others, the decision will be taken higher still, to management (a publisher, perhaps, or an editorial director responsible for the output of the whole publishing house).

The editor is ultimately responsible for the content of the magazine, and usually comes from a journalistic background. The editor's job is to set the parameters for the content (to decide what is and what is not of interest to readers), to commission articles and brief the other full-time staff on the magazine and to ensure that the copy and images delivered by contributors are of a sufficiently high standard for publication.

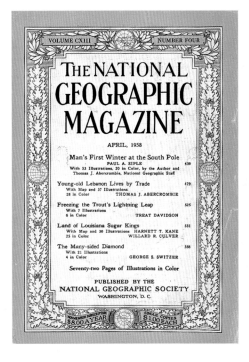

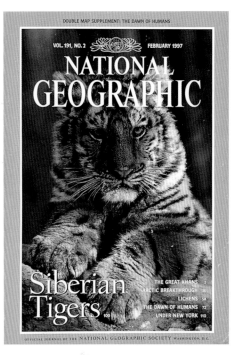

Those working under the editor will have a variety of titles which are imprecise in their meaning: editorial assistant, staff writer, reporter, features writer, senior writer, correspondent, sub-editor, news editor, features editor, associate editor, deputy editor, contributing editor and writer-at-large are all titles which appear frequently in the 'flannel panels' of magazines. For the most part, these titles give some indication of the area of responsibility delegated by the editor to the holder: the features editor, for example, will have particular responsibility for providing features ideas and dealing with features writers. Correspondents, contributing editors and writers-at-large usually have an arrangement with the magazine whereby their knowledge and experience are on tap for the regular staff of the magazine, but they themselves are not employed full-time, allowing them to pursue other interests such as writing for other magazines. The sub-editor is responsible for proof-reading the magazine, checking for stylistic or factual inaccuracies, as well as spelling mistakes or grammatical errors. The sub-editor may also write headlines, standfirsts, captions, re-write badly-fitting copy and even lay out pages where there is no full-time designer to carry out this task.

On top of these full- or part-time contributors, who will usually work in-house at the publisher's office, magazines will often employ freelance journalists, either for their specialist knowledge or because there is not enough work to keep a writer employed full-time.

Overseeing the physical compilation of a magazine is often the job of a production manager or production editor, whose responsibility it is to make sure that all the editorial and advertising content is present and correctly assembled, designed, proofed and printed. It is the production manager, in consultation with the editor and publisher, who sets the production schedules: determining when copy and images will be received, how long the subbing and design processes should take, and when the magazine needs to go to print in order to hit the shops on time. In some instances, the job of production management also falls to the designer.

The main job of the art director or designer, however, is ordering and presenting the material commissioned by the editors and supplied by the journalists, photographers and illustrators, in keeping with the schedules devised by the production manager. Strictly speaking, there is no difference between the jobs performed under the title art director or designer, except that an art director or art editor will occasionally have one or two designers working under them, who actually lay out pages conceived and styled by the art director. The design of a magazine, and by extension its art director, performs a number of functions which must coexist comfortably if the magazine is to work as a whole. These are described in greater detail in later chapters, but

Van
Issue: Oct 1998
Art director:
Fernando Gutiérrez
Spain

suffice it to say here that these usually include making the magazine attractive to potential readers, giving it a distinctive personality or identity, and presenting the content and supplementary information in such a way that readers will find helpful in navigating the magazine.

The working relationships on magazines are enormously important as the best results will only be achieved if the editorial, design and production departments co-operate throughout the process to produce a coherent finished product. An article will work better if the art director commissioning photography has a good understanding of what the editor has commissioned a journalist to write. On most magazines, tight lead times (the period in which the magazine is put together before publication), mean that there is no room for error. Good communication and established working practices are essential.

Where are magazines made?
The image of a newspaper's newsroom is familiar from TV and the movies: a large, open-planned space; a hive of activity, with tens or hundreds of people running about. But since the computerisation of most newspapers over the last ten years, and the advent of devices such as fax and e-mail, today's newspapers employ fewer people in all areas, including the newsroom, and the clatter of typewriters and 'copytakers' taking dictation no longer fills the air. Even so, with very few exceptions, such as *The Economist*, weekly or monthly magazines employ far fewer staff than newspapers, and, with deadlines less frequent, the pace of life is often slower.

As most magazines today are produced using desk top publishing (DTP) packages, a magazine could technically be produced by an individual on a single laptop computer. Indeed, in order to prove this point, the imaging company AGFA organised a stunt in which a magazine was produced by a group on the move in a Volkswagen camper van. Technology has made magazine production a geographically flexible business: the widespread adoption of technologies such as e-mail and large bandwidth digital delivery systems have enabled independent design companies to bid successfully for the job of art directing magazines on a monthly basis. While this has always been possible – and indeed always happened – the ability to pass pages up and down a telephone line has made the process significantly easier and cheaper.

The proliferation of desktop publishing also means that magazines can be produced without many of the skills required a decade or so ago, and in a physically smaller space. Although fanzines and 'amateur' newsletters predate the computer, its introduction has facilitated the production of thousands of magazines in bedrooms and on office PCs after hours, by amateurs who just happen to feel strongly enough about a subject – whether it's football, furniture restoring or Marxism. While it is possible, however, for the individual enthusiast to produce a magazine, most need the input of a variety of skilled individuals in a number of areas – writing, photography, advertising sales, circulation control – to ensure success. Consequently, most magazines are produced within publishing companies by a diverse team of skilled individuals working collaboratively.

Why be a magazine designer?
Like any job, magazine design has its disadvantages. Because of the quick turn around times of magazines, and the financial constraints familiar to most people working in the publishing world, a designer may not be able to spend as much time on a spread or an issue as they would like. Similarly, on some publications, the existence of strict design rules might make parts of the monthly cycle seem tedious or repetitive. But conversely, magazines in general have always acted as a test ground where the latest stylistic innovations are developed before they are adopted by the wider world: David Carson's *Ray Gun* has many imitators in advertising and across all areas of graphic design. *i-D*'s Terry Jones and Lee Swillingham, formerly of *The Face*, are among the many magazine art directors whose pioneering editorial design work has lead to commissions from fashion houses to style advertising campaigns. As the critic Teal Triggs has noted, 'In some cases, magazines are "laboratories of experiment" where innovative art directors and type designers are given the "freedom" to produce visual feasts. Historically, magazines have been the place for the development of new design vocabularies, as well as technical processes.'

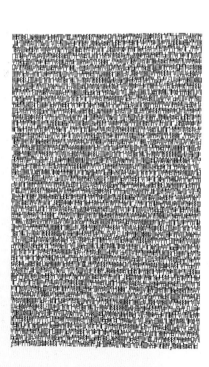

Baseline
Issue: 6, 1985
Art director:
MetaDesign
Germany

Emigré
Issue: 18, 1991
Art director:
Rudy Vanderlans
USA

Ark
Issue: 36,
Summer 1964
Art editors:
Roy Giles and
Stephen Hiett
UK

A Be Sea
Issue: Summer 1993
Produced by:
Bryan Maloney
and Sharon John
UK

Magazines are also 'out there' in the real world, an important part of people's daily lives. Readers form an emotional bond with their favourite titles – both for their content and the way they are presented – and the magazine is consequently one of the few areas where the average person gives any thought to graphic design. Richard Hoggart's seminal study of mass communications, 'The Uses of Literacy' (1957) suggests two things to the modern reader: first, that magazines, unlike newspapers, generally have a short existence. Of the examples quoted by Hoggart – 'titles such as *Secrets*, *Red Star Weekly*, *Lucky Star*, *The Miracle*, *The Oracle*, *Glamour*, *Red Letter* and *Silver Star*' – none exist today. However, even within the archaic titles of these magazines lies a clue to the second point: that magazines are a vivid snapshot of the times in which they were produced – the essence of an era in print form. From the unprecedented, bold colour-bursts of *Nova* and *Twen* in the 1960s to the deconstruction of David Carson's *Ray Gun* in the 1990s, the magazine not only records the concerns of an age upon its pages, but records its visual aesthetic in its design.

The rest of the book

The following chapters look at some of the aspects of editorial design that an art director must contend with, from the way the magazine is bound and dispatched, to the information carried on the cover, the structuring of navigational systems, the use of images and the treatment of text. The diversity of issues raised in these chapters, and in the interviews with established magazine designers which make up the rest of this book, demonstrates the central challenge of magazine design: that the designer's work must do several jobs at once. The magazine must appeal to readers on an aesthetic level, but must be readable; the design framework should be flexible enough to cope with content of all sorts, yet distinctive enough to be identifiable as the property of a particular title; the editorial pages must coexist with advertising, without being overshadowed by it; large amounts of information, such as issue dates, price, subscription information and so on, must be presented in easy-to-use formats, while remaining relatively unobtrusive. The magazines reproduced hereafter – and there are over 100 titles – are not shown as paradigms, but rather are included as examples of the ways in which designers have successfully tackled these problems according to the circumstances in which they find themselves.

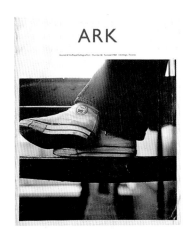

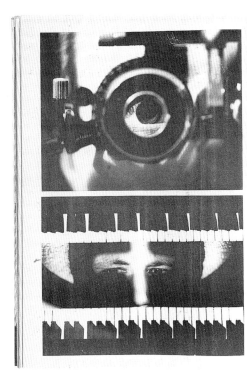

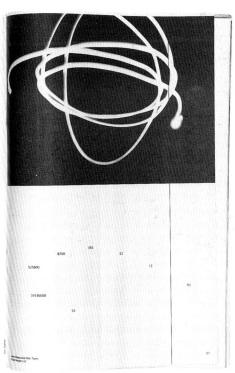

Packaging

Interview
with David Hillman
Front covers
Mastheads
Cover lines
Bar-codes, price and date
Cover images
Cover styles
Cover sets
Guest designers
Spines
Back covers
Binding
Bellybands
Boxes and bags

**Interview
with David Hillman**

David Hillman is one of the world's most successful editorial designers. His career to date has spanned almost four decades, having begun at *The Sunday Times Magazine* in 1962. He has designed and redesigned countless titles both in his home country, the UK, and abroad, including *Design*, *Which?*, *City Limits*, *The New Statesman* and *Society*, *The Guardian newspaper*, *Le Matin* (France) and *People* (US). But it was for the revolutionary women's magazine *Nova* that he first attracted wide attention, and for which he is, in some areas, still best known. Hillman took over the design of *Nova* in 1969, and stayed with the magazine until its demise in 1975. His art directorship coincided with a period of intense social, political and cultural upheaval, and *Nova* not only recorded, but participated in areas of contemporary debate including gender politics and sexual liberation. It confronted contemporary taboos not just through the written word, but through the photographs it commissioned and published.

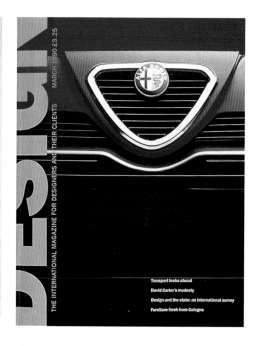

**Cover of
New Statesman
Jun 1998**

**Cover of
Design
Mar 1990**

**Cover of
Nova
Oct 1971**

**Spread from
Nova
Nov 1971**

As well as witnessing great social change, the 11 years that *Nova* existed, from 1964 to 1975, were, without doubt, significant for the development of the magazine publishing industry, as a clutch of titles redefined the concept of the popular magazine and broke new ground in terms of concept, content and appearance. But it is not just the high esteem in which *Nova* is still held that makes it one of Hillman's most treasured design experiences: rather, along with a handful of other projects, *Nova* represents to Hillman the best way in which to produce a magazine, and is a fine example of what happens when design, and the skills of designers, are brought to bear on the message as well as the medium – the content as well as the way it is presented.

So what made *Nova* so special? It is often linked, in histories of magazine publishing, with titles such as *Twen*, *Esquire* and *The Sunday Times Magazine*. All are notable for the way in which design took an unprecedented role not only in defining an identity for the publications, but in suggesting, shaping and expressing content. Willy Fleckhaus, art director of *Twen*, was himself a journalist, while Marc Boxer, who edited *The Sunday Times Magazine*, was best known as a cartoonist, but was as at home with words as he was with pictures. As Hillman, who himself was deputy editor as well as art director of *Nova*, puts it, 'Suddenly you had much more control. A lot of the time magazine art directors are not involved in what the magazine says or how it says it – they're just given pictures to lay out. My position is that writers solve problems with words and designers solve them with pictures and graphics, and there are lots of features where the writer would think, it was a good 5,000-word piece but in fact what it was was a very good photographic essay with long captions. That was how we went about doing *Nova* magazine: it wasn't an "us and them" situation.'

The extent to which Hillman, as a designer, was able to influence the editorial content and stance on *Nova* was in some part determined by his experiences before joining the magazine. He had started his working life on *The Sunday Times Magazine*, attracted into publishing straight from college by the 'much more exciting things' being done at magazines such as the UK's *Town*, Germany's *Twen*, and *Esquire* and *Harper's Bazaar* in the US, than were coming out of the corporate design studios. His belief, shared by many other editorial designers, is that 'the great thing about editorial design, be it on a newspaper or a magazine, is that you can take risks, and you might make a mistake. On a daily newspaper you live with it for three or four hours. On a weekly you live with it for a month and on a monthly you live with it for three months, but at least you can try things.'

At *The Sunday Times Magazine*, Marc Boxer was at the forefront of a movement to change the design content of magazines, creating new ways of telling stories through evocative images and arresting layouts. As Hillman describes it: 'Marc Boxer was probably the first one... whose design knowledge actually made the magazine. *The Sunday Times Magazine* had a high design content because he had an interest in words and pictures. He made it possible for others, such as myself later on at *Nova* magazine to be deputy editor as well as art editor. Art direction is something where to do the role properly, you have to be aware of both words and pictures.'

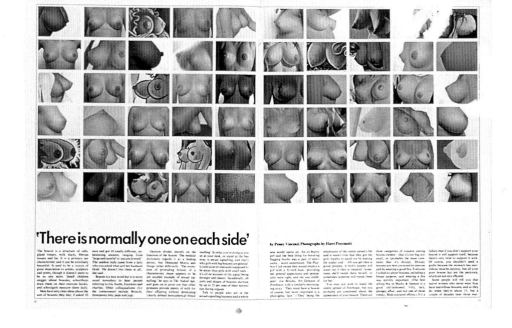

In 1965 Hillman left *The Sunday Times Magazine* with Boxer to launch a new magazine, *London Life*, which combined a listings guide to London events with features on the artistic luminaries of the day. In retrospect, Hillman feels, it was probably too far ahead of its time, and it soon closed. He returned to *The Sunday Times*, this time to design the reviews section within the newspaper and edit a 'Design for Living' section – his first direct engagement with the written word. When *Nova* magazine's art director, Harri Peccinotti, left in 1969, the stage was set for Hillman to put what he had learned about the interplay of words, pictures and design to use on *Nova*.

Nova was intended by its publishers IPC to be an intelligent magazine for women – as Hillman describes it in relation to a rival title: '*Cosmopolitan* was about how to get your man and keep him, and *Nova* was about how to keep your man but retain your self respect.' In keeping with the spirit of the times, its editors, art directors and contributors challenged conventions and taboos at almost every turn: issues relating to race, sexuality, gender relations and politics were openly discussed, alongside fashion and beauty features. 'It was very much pushing the boundaries of what the public was used to accepting in a magazine,' remembers Hillman. 'So all the taboos were discussed openly. The word "fuck" was used – in the right context...'

Correspondingly, the magazine's design broke new ground with almost every issue, from its rejection of a neat list of coverlines up the left-hand side of the cover ('I think that people simply won't read them – so my way was to put across one strong concept which you hoped would intrigue people') to the role taken by the art director in determining the 'message' or argument of a particular feature. *Nova* was heavily reliant on photography, and Hillman recognised that an art director can commission a 'story' from a photographer in the same way that an editor might from a writer: 'You can visually change a story just by the way you select the pictures,' he says now. 'There were times when I sat down with the photographer and the fashion editor and wrote story lines: we would write a little film script of what would happen on each spread – it was a means of creating a flow. We had a similar idea when we did studio shoots, and there were occasions when we had gone off with the intention to do a really high-style fashion thing and then ended up using the one lucky shot – because there's always one shot from a shoot that's a million miles from what the intent was. And you can do the same with reportage.' In its use of photographs, *Nova* again broke boundaries: it was the first magazine to publish Helmut Newton's famous nudes, for example, and regularly made images the centrepiece of written articles, rather than supplementary information. In other instances, the photographer was allowed their own 'point of view' on a story, even where it differed from that of the writer – an editorial decision made by the art director: 'One of the big issues between writers and art directors is that if you don't read the copy, the pictures can have a totally different editorial stance to the text,' explains Hillman. 'But sometimes we said, "OK, this is what the photographer's view of the story is, and this is what the writer's is". The two can have different perspectives.'

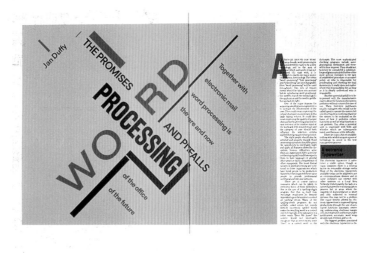

Spread from
New Statesman

Cover of
Nova
Sep 1973

Cover of
Nova
Jan 1975

Spread from
Nova
Mar 1975

By the mid-70s the first boom of the counter-culture revolution was over, giving way to a period of economic hardship in the UK. *Nova*'s uncompromising position, and eclectic mix of interests had not endeared it to advertisers anyway – as Hillman puts it, 'media buyers have pigeon holes for brains... they want to be able to target one thing' – and its publishers decided to close it down. But as Hillman observes in retrospect, 'The further away I get from *Nova* magazine the more I can see that it had reached the end of its life. The more taboos that we confronted, the more it became acceptable for other magazines to follow suit. And in the end we ran out of taboos.'

Since 1975, Hillman has designed and redesigned magazines and newspapers on a freelance basis (since 1978 as a partner of the international design consultancy Pentagram). Working out-of-house on magazines has meant that there have been fewer opportunities to become involved with the magazine in its entirety, as he had done at *Nova*: 'What I find hard about doing editorial jobs here [Pentagram],' he explains, 'is that you are separated from the guts of the magazine. They come in and what they want to buy is your style, your intuitiveness about how pictures sit on pages. But I find it very difficult to separate myself from the words – I feel quite critical about the final product. The most successful jobs for me are the ones where you are taken in to the belly of the magazine; that's why *The Guardian* was so successful – I had a very close relationship with [the newspaper's editor] Peter Preston, and I understood the thinking behind everything that was done in the newspaper.'

While there have been instances where Hillman was able to identify with the staff and content of a magazine – for instance, at the *The New Statesman* and *Society* where he was 'working with a bunch of people who felt very strongly about the history of the magazine' – working at a distance from the internal workings of a publishing operation has rarely been as satisfying as full immersion, and as he explains, has impacted on the overall quality of the product: 'The worst thing is "Here's our magazine, can you restyle it." I do it, and people say – "Oh, that spread looks good," and you say "Yes, it looks good, but it's got nothing to do with what the article is all about." Templates lead to parrot-fashion design.' For David Hillman, at least, art direction is not about establishing a grid, or styling a masthead, or even about a good-looking juxtaposition of image and text. In its best form, it involves the art director having a full and in-depth understanding of what the magazine says, and through design, influencing how it is said.

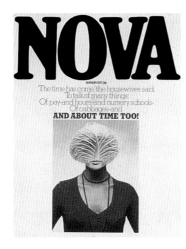

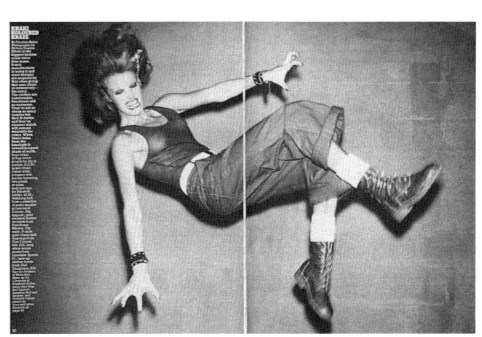

The magazine cover is a subject art directors, editors and publishers treat with almost neurotic seriousness. For a magazine facing fierce competition from its neighbours on the rack, it is the difference between being 15 per cent up on average sales in any given month, and 15 per cent down. Of course, content is the key, but without a good cover to attract their attention in the first place, readers will never know what was inside. In his novel *With Friends Like These*, managing director of Condé Nast UK, Nicholas Coleridge, describes the process of selecting a cover for magazines very like those he oversees in real life (*Vogue*, *GQ*, *Homes and Gardens*): 'Successful cover personalities are difficult to predict. A Hollywood star can put out an Oscar-winning performance but flop on a cover. A different star might be going through a professional famine but still shift magazines. Certain actors like Kevin Costner, Hugh Grant, Michael Caine

and Johnny Depp always sell. They're bankers. Barabra Streisand's a banker. Roseanne Barr's a banker. Uma Thurman too. Elizabeth Hurley does it for a certain title but not for others. Kate Moss works where Elizabeth Hurley doesn't. Princess Diana was once worth a 15 per cent boost but then it stopped working. Oprah Winfrey doesn't even pass go. You learn these things as you go along.'

The magazines Coleridge is describing are monthly glossies, in close competition for readers – and by extensive advertising revenue and financial survival – with several other all-but-identical titles. The cover is critical in persuading the reader to pick up one magazine instead of another from the rack. Even when the magazine is not a high-profile, mass-market glossy – a subscription only or in-house magazine, for example – the cover must still compete for the

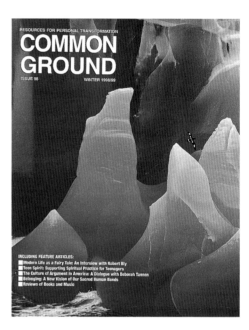

Eye
Issue: 29, 1998
Art director:
Nick Bell
UK

Common Ground
Issue: 98, 1998
Art director:
Alan Cummings
USA

Dazed & Confused
Issue: Aug 1997
Art director:
Matt Roach
UK

Crash
Issue: 5, 1998
Art director:
Yorgo
France

Although this San Franciso publication is distributed free on street corners, and is produced on a low budget, an impactful colour cover is used to attract the passer-by's attention away from other distractions.

In this issue, cover model Helena Christiansen's modesty was preserved by the application of a metallic coating. Half of the readers who bought the magazine and scratched off the panel got lucky, and saw Christiansen unclothed. The others were disappointed to find her sensored by two black stars under the panel.

reader's attention with everything around it: whatever else is in the magazine rack, in the mail that day, or being distributed on the street corner.

Covers have other responsibilities too, besides attracting attention and shifting copies, as Nicholas Coleridge implies in *With Friends Like These*: 'If circulation directors were editors you'd only get six cover personalities on a loop, round and round again. Except at Christmas where there'd be a heavily decorated Christmas tree with sprigs of holly around the logo. And all the cover lines would be about sex and relationships and there wouldn't be any green logos or blue backgrounds because they don't sell. And all the fashion models would be blond and smiling and wearing red jackets and be called Claudia Schiffer.' Readers expect a familiar framework and new content

when they read each new issue of a magazine. As well as creating a long-term brand impression, the cover must also convince the reader that what they are being asked to pay for one month is substantially different to what they paid for the month before, and substantially different again from the next magazine in the rack.

The interrelated functions of the cover – provision of basic information such as price, bar-code, issue number, month, name of magazine, what's inside, special offers, as well as the aforementioned aesthetic considerations – are discussed individually over the coming pages. But magazine covers work as a whole, and successful cover designers consider each of these aspects in the context of all of the others.

DAZED & CONFUSED

THIRD ANNIVERSARY SPECIAL
FASHION ISSUE

ONLY £1

INSTANT WIN SCRATCH & SEE

STARRING:
NOBUYOSHI ARAKI
NICK KNIGHT
HELENA CHRISTENSEN
DAVID LACHAPELLE
KARL LAGERFELD
GLEN LUCHFORD
RAYMOND MEIER
STEVEN MEISEL
JEAN BAPTISTE MONDINO
HELMUT NEWTON
DAVID SIMS
MARIO SORRENTI
JUERGEN TELLER
MARIO TESTINO

PHIL BICKER
ANNA COCKBURN
KATY ENGLAND
TIBOR KALMAN
CATHY KASTERINE
RICHARD PANDISCIO
NANCY ROHDE
CARINE ROITFELD
CHRISTOPH STEINEGGER
VENETIA SCOTT
LEE SWILLINGHAM
MELANIE WARD
ALEX WHITE
CAMILLE BIDAULT-
WADDINGTON

33 SCRATCH & SEE
AUG 1997 UK £1.00 US$4.95

crash

KRUDER & DORFMEISTER   VERSATILE   DAN SIMMONS
DETROIT DIGITALE RESISTANCE   CASSIUS   SUBLIME
PLANETE JEU_BIENVENUE DANS UN MONDE REEL

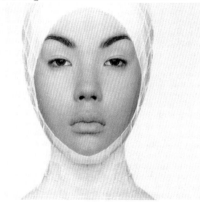

18.19

Among better known magazines, the shape of the letterforms that make up the masthead are almost as familiar as the name itself. This is particularly true of magazines which have existed in more or less the same form for many years: over time, the mastheads of *Vogue* and *Esquire* have achieved iconic status in the same way as the logos of Coca-Cola or IBM. Paradoxically, when mastheads achieve icon status, magazine designers are given a degree of flexibility in their implementation: rules are there to be broken. In the example shown on page 22, the 'G' from *Vogue* has been substituted for Kate Moss' face, yet the magazine is still unmistakably *Vogue*.

Esquire's masthead has been subtly redrawn since the magazine's design heyday under the likes of George Lois in the 1950s and 1960s, but its character is preserved. Other globally famous faces include *Life* and *Billboard*, both of which have changed little or not at all since the magazines were founded over half a century ago.

Most mastheads are fixed designs. Colours may change, or perhaps even sizes, but the lettering itself remains the same from issue to issue. Some magazines, however, ignore this convention: *Blah Blah Blah*, influenced by its sister title *Ray Gun*, changed its masthead with each issue, and yet remained distinctive and recognisable – a tribute to the qualities of the design itself.

Under other circumstances, the use of a flexible masthead would have meant a missed opportunity for the designers. *Loaded* magazine's masthead works hard as a signature for the title: as well as appearing on the cover, the distinctive logotype appears in bold within the text of the magazine whenever the name *Loaded* appears. This stylistic device is in keeping with the journalistic approach of the magazine, based on the 'new journalism' of the 1960s, as practiced by Hunter S Thompson, Tom Wolfe and others. Not only does the reporter frequently figure in the story, but they often become the subject of the article. By using the magazine's bold masthead in the copy in such

Blah Blah Blah
Issues: Apr, May,
Jun, Jul 1996
Art director:
Substance
UK

Blah Blah Blah's
designers changed its
masthead every issue,
not just by moving around
the cover, but by altering
its actual make-up.

Esquire
Issue: Feb 1999
Art director:
Christophe Gowans
UK

Typographische
Monatsblätter
Issue: 1958
Switzerland

Immerse
Issue: 001, 1996
Art director:
Struktur Design
UK

This masthead is a
typographic play on the
name of the magazine,
appearing to be half-
submerged.

instances, the design implicitly draws attention to this fact. This neat example of design supporting the editorial proposition of a title would not have been possible if the designers had created a masthead that did not sit comfortably within the text, or varied from issue to issue.

A novel approach to mastheads was employed by Atelier Works when the design studio redesigned the UK Design Council's journal, *Design*. The word 'design' was written into the main cover line of each issue, effectively combining the functions of masthead and cover line. Furthermore, it is not too far-fetched to argue that the integrated masthead suggests that the magazine itself is at the centre of design issues. In this case, the magazine is principally distributed through subscription, so the masthead does not have to do the job of identifying the magazine at a glance to potential purchasers (although picking the word 'design' out in red means that it could arguably do that job too).

Such magazines are free to be more subtle with their mastheads, using smaller type or playing the sort of games that make the cover of *Design* so effective. Whether the magazine sells from a news-stand, by subscription or is handed out on street corners, though, the masthead is important: a masthead is a magazine's signature.

VOGUE

APRIL
£3.00

**SUMMER'S
BEST BUY**
THE LIGHT
COAT

SEX
WITH
THE
EX

**THE BEAUTIFUL
AND THE DAMNED
KENYA'S NEW
BOHEMIANS**

**LIV
TYLER**
THE COOLEST
STAR IN TOWN

**PASHMINA
TROUSERS?**
CLOTHES YOU
NEVER KNEW
YOU NEEDED

Kate Moss
AN ICON BARES ALL

for men who should know better   MAY 1999 £2.80

loaded

61ST ISSUE
SPECTACULAR!
FEATURING THE TOP 61
loaded ICONS OF THE '90s
AS VOTED FOR BY US

FREE
POSTER
& GATEFOLD
COVER

*CATHERINE ZETA JONES, TIGER WOODS,
MADONNA, THE FAST SHOW, KATE MOSS, TONY ADAMS,
OASIS, MILLA JOVOVICH and PIPER THE THIN OX*

plus
ELECTRONIC,
KEITH ALLEN ON FULHAM,
LENNOX LEWIS: THE TRUTH,
CHRIS MORRIS & PETER COOK,
BASEMENT JAXX
AND THE WORLD AT RANDOM

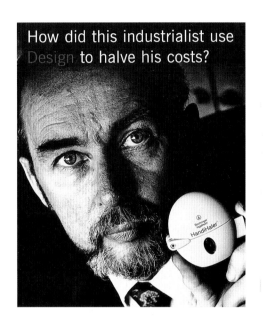

How did this industrialist use Design to halve his costs?

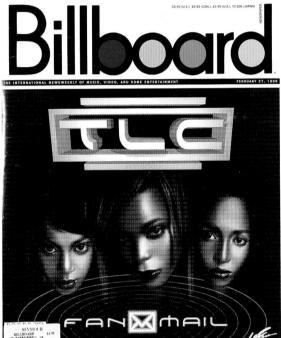

$5.95 (U.S.), $6.95 (CAN.), £4.95 (U.K.), Y2,500 (JAPAN)

Billboard

THE INTERNATIONAL NEWSWEEKLY OF MUSIC, VIDEO, AND HOME ENTERTAINMENT   FEBRUARY 27, 1999

ADVERTISEMENT

MALAYSIA
The Anwar Verdict

NATO AT 50
The alliance fights its first war

Vogue
Issue: Apr 1999
Art director:
Robin Derrick
UK

The elegant serifs of
Vogue's masthead are
instantly familiar, and are
employed on versions of
the magazine all over the
world. In this instance,
the general public's
familiarity with the logo
allows the designer to
sacrifice the 'G' in order
to obtain the desired
cover image.

Loaded
Issue: 61, 1999
Art director:
Jon Link
UK

Design
Issue: Spring 1995
Art director:
Atelier Works
UK

Billboard
Issue: Feb 1999
USA

The *Billboard* masthead,
with its colour-filled
counter spaces, is a
unique and distinctive
icon whose recognition
factor far exceeds the
number of readers the
magazine actually has.

Time
Issue: Apr 1999
Art director:
Paul Lussier
USA

The primary function of cover lines is to draw readers in, to persuade them to buy one magazine instead of its competitor. Even when the magazine is effectively pre-sold – as in the case of a subscription-only title or newspaper supplement – cover lines will often be added, either to encourage readers to read what they have bought or just to fulfil their expectations of what a magazine should look like.

The treatment of information on the cover varies from title to title, in order to achieve a variety of effects: a restrained approach, in which only the major features are trailed, might suggest a quiet sophistication while; covers that breathlessly announce every last product review or horoscope page may be attempting to suggest that the magazine is a bargain – 'all this and a TV listings guide too'.

Every issue of every magazine has its unique selling points – a big interview or the results of a major survey – and in those instances, the designer will use text size or colour to allow the relevant cover lines to stand out not just against the magazine's competitors on the news-stand, but against the other lines on the same cover.

The way cover lines are written also give uninitiated readers a clue to the personality of the magazine. They might be chatty, informative, witty or sensational. The same is true for the way the lines are typographically styled: with nothing better to go on, readers will look for visual clues in the graphic language of the cover – does the magazine look like an easy/entertaining/ useful read?

Cover lines, like information carried on the spine, can also be used to add value indirectly: in magazines that are likely to be kept for future reference, a designer might organise the cover lines in a way likely to assist the reader with finding a particular report or article at a later date. Graphic devices to consider in such situations might include a regular formula or template for the presentation of information, to facilitate the reader's search.

Ultimately, for the designer to produce effective cover lines, they must consider not only the cover image – whether the lines should be run around a central figure, or buried near the edge of the page, fight for attention with the masthead or take a humble second place – but also the content and personality of the magazine itself.

 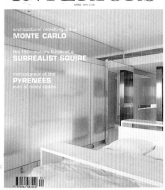  

**The World of Interiors
Issue: Apr 1999
(subscription version)
Art director:
Malgosia Szemberg
UK**

**The World of Interiors
Issue: Apr 1999
(news-stand version)
Art director:
Malgosia Szemberg
UK**

**The Editor
Issue: Apr 1999
Art director:
Simon Esterson
UK**

**Frieze
Issue: Dec 1992
Art director:
TG · nashnille
UK**

As has been seen, the cover principally carries information designed to persuade the potential reader to peruse or buy the magazine; in their own way, mastheads, cover images and cover lines are all designed to present an attractive package to the reader. However, the cover must also carry certain additional information which, although it makes no claims for the contents of the magazine, does assist the reader with its purchase: the issue date, price and bar-code. As these pieces of information do not add to the magazine's fundamental proposition of being an interesting read, a useful source of information or a pleasant diversion, it is unlikely that the cover designer will want to make a feature of them. But as they are required, they must also be incorporated into the cover design in such a way that they do not detract from the work done by the other elements with which they share the space.

The trickiest to handle is perhaps the bar-code, as its white background means that it appears incongruous next to the cover image. The designers of *Big* magazine have chosen to make a feature of this, positioning the bar-code around the cover in a seemingly random

manner. The designers of *Life*, however, place all of the supplementary information together in a neat box under the masthead.

While in some cases the price of a magazine may act as an incentive to buy, the reader will usually be able to guess roughly what the magazine costs, and the actual amount is largely irrelevant when they decide whether or not to buy it. Nevertheless, the price must be immediately apparent for the convenience of the seller, if nothing else.

The issue date is important: readers reasonably like to feel that they are buying the most up-to-date issue of a magazine. The publisher must decide whether the magazine is to adopt a sequential numbering system, or identify the issue by date of publication. Both systems have their merits as a sequential numbering system will convey the age, and by extension, the authority of the magazine, if this is a source of pride to its owners and readers, while a date-based system allows the contents of the magazine to be more easily associated with a specific point in time if the magazine is referred to at a later date.

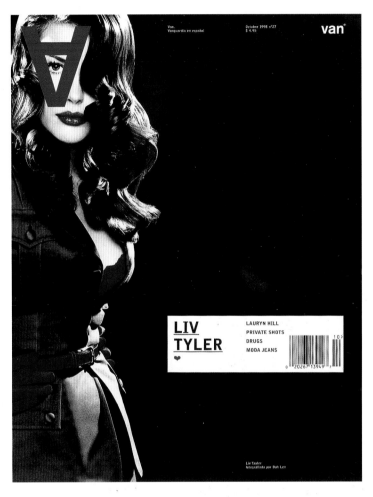

Van
Issue: Oct 98
Art director:
Fernando Gutiérrez
Spain

Life
Issue: Feb 1999
USA

GQ
Issue: May 99
Art director:
Tony Chambers
UK

Big
Issue: 20
Art director:
Douglas Lloyd
USA

It is stating the obvious to observe that most magazines today, with a few notable exceptions, carry cover images. But this was not always the case. Today, only a few news weeklies carry text-based stories on the front pages in the style of a daily newspaper. Until very recently this practice was far more widespread: *The Spectator*, which led with text on the front page as recently as the 1960s, now has its own distinctive cover style, based around its use of cartoons and illustration.

Similarly, it may seem superfluous to say that the image displayed on the cover changes with each issue, but this in itself is an innovation. A hundred and fifty years ago, covers were generally seen as nothing more than protective wraps for magazines, and while the information carried thereon obviously varied from issue to issue, publishers saw no need to change the image on a regular basis. As Patricia Frantz Kery

pointed out in her book *Great Magazine Covers of the World*, 'The Strand, for instance, used the same street illustration for several decades, only updating now and then by replacing a horse-drawn carriage with an automobile when they could no longer avoid it'. Even today, among the consumer glossies, there is so little variation of cover image as to make it almost irrelevant. These formulaic magazine covers are now little more than code – visual shorthand for the type of feature one might expect to find inside.

Nevertheless, art directors, editors and publishers agonise over cover shots, which are believed to have an enormous influence on sales. Selection of exactly the right shot is seen by some not only as an art, but also as something of a science: in the 1960s the magazine publishing company Condé Nast undertook some research into what made a winning cover and concluded that, among other things, creating eye

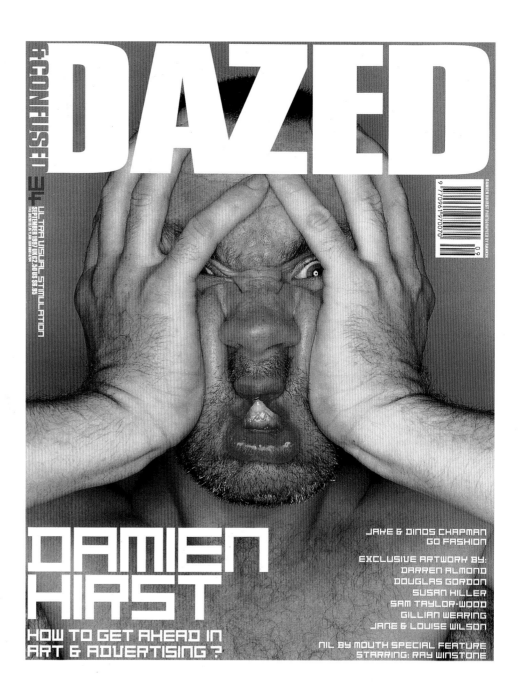

contact between the purchaser (of either sex) and an attractive woman on the cover was a surefire way to shift magazines. Judging by the success the company enjoys today, and its continued adherence to this formula, nothing has happened in the interim to dissuade it of this view. Similarly, *Paris Match*'s research shows that cover shots of celebrities sell better than politicians.

Whether it's a celebrity, politician, or unknown model, male or female, among the mass-market glossies, the most common cover image is the head or body shot. A casual glance at the news stand will show that most consumer magazines, whether targeted at men or women, feature a woman on the cover. Exceptions are found in news and special interest publications. It is possible, however, to subvert the dominant paradigm, and use an unusual head shot to create an outstanding cover, as magazines like the issue *Dazed & Confused* shown here demonstrate.

Today's trade titles usually attempt to represent some aspect of the magazine's content in an interesting or attractive way on the cover – a computer magazine, for example, might feature a digitally manipulated shot of a monitor, mouse or keyboard.

In the case of news-based magazines, the cover image has also traditionally acted as a record of the most significant event of the week or month. To a certain extent, this function has been supplanted by television in the last few decades. But television is impermanent: pictures disappear at the same speed as they arrive – in fractions of a second. A collage of the collected covers of *Time* magazine would be as evocative a pictorial history of America's 20th century as you could hope to get, and it was exactly this image that the magazine used to promote its unique position in the history of publishing in a recent advertising campaign. The fact that the surrounding material - the masthead, the red border – have changed so little over the years, only serves to amplify the uniqueness of each image when they are seen together.

Whether the magazine is a trade title, a consumer glossy, a newspaper supplement or a news weekly, there are essentially two types of cover image: most magazine covers today feature a simple, 'icon' shot (of either a person or an object) which can be understood at a glance and appreciated at length. Into the second category fall the more complex, detailed images which require some study before they can be understood or appreciated. Examples include the illustrated covers of *The New Yorker* or the cartoon covers of the satirical magazine *Private Eye*, where the reader must scan the photograph, read the text, and then look back at the photograph before getting the joke. In deciding which route to go down, the designer must take into account the importance of an instant reaction in the reader's decision whether or not to buy the magazine, potential conflicts with other elements such as cover lines and the suitability of the image to the personality of the magazine itself.

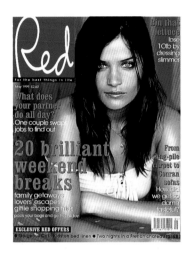

Dazed & Confused
Issue: 34
Art director:
Matt Roach
UK

Red
Issue: May 1999
Art director:
Geoff Waring
UK

Time
Issue: Jan 1961
USA

Elle
Issue: Jun 1999
Art director:
Jo Sams
UK

The New Yorker
Issue: Feb 1939
USA

Frieze
Issue: Apr 1994
Art director:
H. Crumb & Crumb
UK

Private Eye
Issue: May 1999
Editor: Ian Hislop
UK

RSA Journal
Issue: 2 | 4 1998
Art director:
Mike Dempsey
UK

The Spectator
Issue: Jun 1999
Cover illustration:
Michael Heath
UK

Cover styles

The difference between a themed 'set' or series of magazine covers is small but significant. While the 'sets' described in the next few pages may run for a few issues, some magazines make a 'trademark' of using a particular type or style of cover image. Over time this becomes as recognisable a feature of the magazine's cover as its masthead. *The New Yorker*, for example, always uses illustration on its cover. Likewise, *Twen*, the German 1960s magazine art directed by Willy Fleckhaus, always used a colour shot of a beautiful girl or multiple girls, set within a black border. The design does not look remarkable today, but this is principally because it has been widely copied ever since. The UK fashion and style magazine *i-D* has a subtle and unusual cover style: its art director, editor and publisher Terry Jones noticed that the magazine's masthead, which runs vertically down the page, looked a little like a smiling, winking face. Consequently, all cover stars, from models and film stars to designers and musicians, are depicted winking.

i-D
Issues: Nov 1993,
Jan 1994, Feb 1999
Art director:
Terry Jones
UK

Twen
Issues: Oct 1965,
Oct 1966, Jan 1966,
Mar 1966, Jul 1962
Art director:
Willy Fleckhaus
Germany

twen

Nr. 10 Oktober 1965 7. Jahr 2,– DM 1 H 6773 E

So ist das mit der Eifersucht

Da steckt Musik in diesem Heft: die Knef (schau)spielt Schlager der 20er Jahre • Balletts tanzen über phantastische Farbseiten (zum Ausklappen und Aufhängen) • Und Nana Mouskouri (ja richtig: Sonntags nie) tönt von der neuen twen-Schallplatte • Sie erfahren, wie in diesem Herbst gut angezogene Mädchen aussehen • Sie erleben, wie der Mini Cooper S uns den Spaß am Autofahren wiedergibt • Und Sie lesen den ungeheuerlichen Bericht über ein unerfreuliches, diskretes Entbindungsheim für ledige Mädchen

twen

Nr. 10 Oktober 1966 8. Jahr DM 2,20 ÖS. 15,– sfrs. 2,50 Lire 450,– B 6773 E

Ist Verlobung verlorene Zeit ?

Mädchen, die Karriere machen !

Wo holen sie die Männer her ?

twen

Nr. 1 Januar 1966 8. Jahr 2,– DM 1 H 6773 E

Lieben ohne treu zu sein?

In diesem Heft gibt's viel zu lesen: Françoise Sagans Roman „Gute Nacht, Liebe" • Interview mit Federico Fellini • Alle Filmtricks in Bonds Thunderball • Gespräche in Ost-Berlin • Und zum Anschauen: Ein Irving-Penn-Foto zum Aufhängen • Viele herrliche Gläser zum Austrinken

twen

Nr. 3 März 1966 8. Jahr 2,20 DM 1 H 6773 E

Ehemann oder Liebhaber Was hilft den Frauen weiter?

twen

1 H 6773 E Nr. 7 1966 4. Jahr

nimmt die Leuwerik aufs Korn

Ruth reitet auf Bambi

Because of the blandness of many magazine covers, it would be easy to assume that they look similar because of a shared aesthetic, rather than an uneasiness about non-conformity. Some magazines, however, make a feature of a distinctive cover style, running over a series of issues. This may be based on the style of a photographer, or a particular subject matter. In these instances, the covers 'make sense' when seen individually or together. The style becomes identifiably the property of a particular title, and help to create a sense of continuity between issues. They are also an opportunity for an art director to explore a particular idea, theme or subject matter at length and from several different angles.

**Graphics
International
Issues: 59, 60,
58, 57, 52
Cover art direction:
Struktur Design
UK**

DESIGN

THE INTERNATIONAL MAGAZINE FOR DESIGNERS AND THEIR CLIENTS

JULY 1992 £3.95

3.058

058

Meisterburo

Information design special:

Signs and swingometers

Getting across Berlin

Richard Wurman: phenomenon

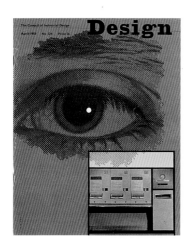   

Design Issue dates and art directors:	**Jul 1992** Maureen Jenkins	**Apr 1959** Kenneth Garland	**Dec 1959** Kenneth Garland cover by Ernest Hock	**Mar 1960** Kenneth Garland cover by Foster	**Apr 1964** Brian Grimbly cover by Anthony Froshaug
		Mar 1963 Brian Grimbly cover by Kenneth Garland	**Sept 1963** Brian Grimbly	**Spring 1998** Stephen Coates	**Spring 1999** Alexander Boxill

immerse
sound(e)scapes

autechre
tomato v underworld
meat beat manifesto
staalplaat
download
jenny randles

immerse
sound(e)scapes

alter ego
blast first.disobay
t.power
witchman
v23

immerse
sound(e)scapes

techno
ambient
atmospherica
industrial
noise
jazz
electronica
fortuona
graphics
film
print

biosphere
bowery electric
the designers republic
locust
christopher priest

IMM 003 | £2.75

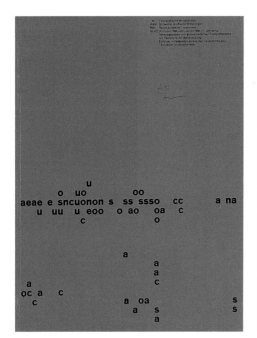
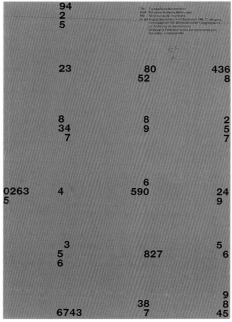
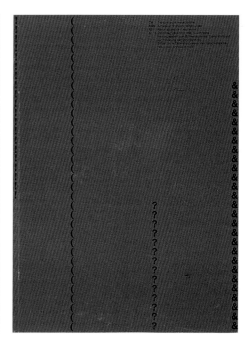

Immerse
Issues:
001 (1996)
002 (1997)
003 (1997)
Art director:
Struktur Design
UK

Typographische
Monasblätter
Issues: Jun/Jul,
Aug/Sept and
Dec 1958
Switzerland

It is not uncommon for the design of a magazine's cover to be contracted out, so to speak; an art director may do this in order to make use of a skill or style that is unique to the guest designer – readers may be surprised to learn that Matisse, Picasso, Toulouse-Lautrec, Miró, Chagall, Dalí, Braque, Klimt, Duchamp, Rockwell and Disney (as in Walt) are among the legion of artists who have designed magazine covers at one time or another. Today, well-known graphic designers such as Alan Fletcher and Tibor Kalman, who have both designed the cover of the Italian magazine *Domus*, would often be drafted in to give magazines a touch of their distinctive style, whether on a single issue or

over a run of issues. Some – including *Big* and *Immerse* – also turn over several interior spreads in each issue to guest designers

The guest designer differs from the photographer or illustrator commissioned to produce a specific cover image in that they are given a free hand to produce the cover they feel is appropriate. Furthermore, if they are already an established artist or designer, their distinctive style, or the mere knowledge that they designed the cover, may add to the magazine's credibility in the eye of the reader.

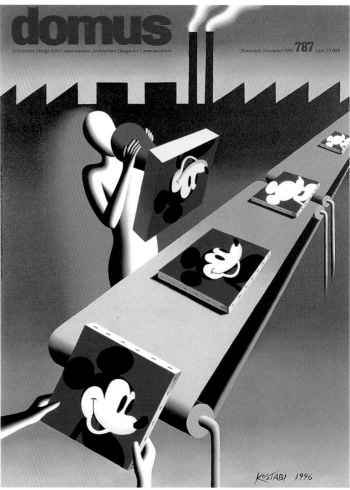

Nikkei Design
Guest designer:
Angus Hyland
Japan

This Japanese design magazine regularly invites well-known designers from around the world to produce a short run of covers. The example shown here is one of a run of twelve by British designer Angus Hyland, which ran throughout 1999.

Domus
Issue: Nov 1996
Guest designer:
Mark Kostabi
Italy

Design
Issue: Oct 1962
Guest designer:
Fletcher/Forbes/Gill
UK

For a long period, a different designer was invited to create the cover of each issue of the UK Design Council's journal *Design*.

du
Issue: Apr 1977
Guest designer:
Jean Tinguely
Switzerland

The form of binding used on any magazine will in part be decided by the number of pages it contains, in part by budgetary considerations, and in part by such factors as how durable the magazine needs to be. The majority of news-stand magazines contain hundreds of pages and are perfect bound, leaving a small, flat surface between the front and back covers which is all too often ignored – the spine.

The spine can be important in a number of ways: it can carry identifying marks, such as the logo and issue number, thereby allowing the reader to find a particular magazine from within a flat stack (although magazines, unlike books, are usually sold with their covers facing outwards from the shelf, they are usually stacked flat by readers).

Similarly, the spine can carry an abbreviated list of contents, allowing the reader to access a specific feature in a particular magazine within a collection.

Eye magazine, for example, carries information about its main features on the spine, adding to the perception that the magazine has on-going use as a reference source, and that it will be kept after reading rather than disposed of. This is a helpful perception both for readers and, to a lesser extent, potential advertisers to have of the magazine. Likewise, *Sky* magazine carries the month, year and the name of the cover star, by which information it is presumed the issue can be identified. The information carried on the spines of individual magazines can also help to create a sense of narrative, or continuity, when seen in the context of a series of issues. When consecutive issues of *Loaded* magazine are stacked together, for example, a picture appears, made up of 'abstract' fragments of the image that appear on individual spines. In this way readers are encouraged to think of each issue of the magazine as part of a series.

These small details contribute to a representation of the magazine not as a one-off purchase, but as a brand which encourages loyalty and regular consumption.

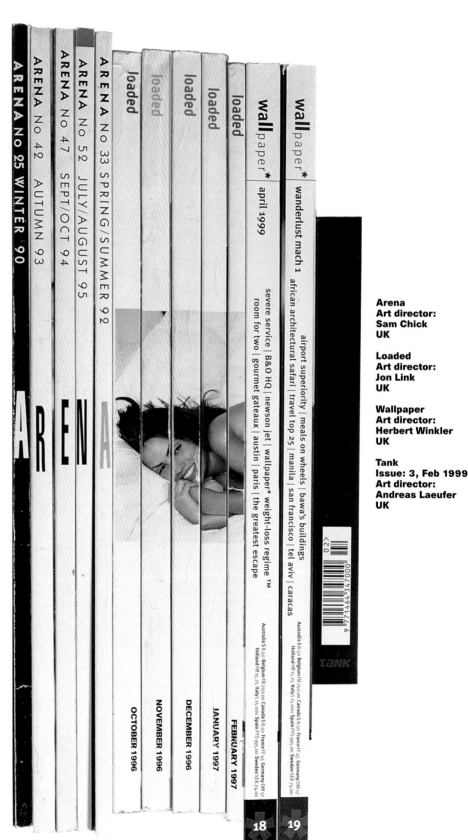

Arena
Art director:
Sam Chick
UK

Loaded
Art director:
Jon Link
UK

Wallpaper
Art director:
Herbert Winkler
UK

Tank
Issue: 3, Feb 1999
Art director:
Andreas Laeufer
UK

Front covers are to magazines what petals are to flowers: they attract attention, and then lure visitors to what is really important – the nectar inside. Spines have a function: they identify the magazine on the shelf, or in a collection. But back covers are usually considered surplus to requirements, in terms of promoting the magazine and identifying its contents, which is why they are normally sold to advertisers, who will pay increased rates for such a prominent position. Some magazines, however, do choose to forgo that extra revenue in order to make a feature out of the back cover. *Creative Review* not only uses its inside back cover (for competitions), but also utilises the whole space offered by the wrapping of the magazine – spine, front and back cover – for the

reproduction of an image; *Dazed & Confused* gives its readers two front covers for the price of one, printing a second image upside-down on the back of the magazine, together with masthead and cover lines; *Eye* magazine uses its back cover to trail the contents of the issue; *Design* magazine, which as the journal of the UK's Design Council, does not take advertising anyway, uses its reverse face to provide information on a particularly interesting product. But the use of back covers for editorial purposes goes beyond functionality; as long as the majority of magazines run advertising on the back cover, those that don't will enjoy the distinction of difference, giving readers another small reason to covet, value and admire their magazine.

**Dazed & Confused
Issue: Feb 1999
Art director:
Matt Roach
UK**

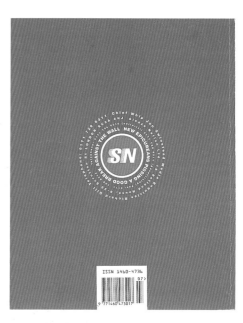

F100
Issue: vol 01 no. 03
Art director:
Faber & Wildschidtz
Denmark

Eye
Issue: 31, 1999
Art director:
Nick Bell
UK

Creative Review
Issue: Sep 1998
Art director:
Nathan Gale
UK

Design
Issue: Spring 1995
Art director:
Atelier Works
UK

sleazenation
Issue: Jul/Aug 1998
Art director:
Guerilla6
UK

For a number of very good reasons – cost (departing from the norm is usually expensive), convention, durability (magazines that must endure a month on the news-stands, for example, need a high level of rigidity), and ease of use – most magazines are designed to be read in portrait format, bound down the left hand edge. Of course, a minority of magazines come in unusual shapes and sizes, and others use unconventional binding methods; some of these are considered over the next few pages. However, most magazine designers, whether for reasons of cost, conditions of sale or merely stylistic preference, will opt for conventional binding. Even within what might be considered 'conventional' binding, a number of alternatives are available to the designer, each with

its own merits. Factors such as the number of pages will determine the binding method most appropriate to the publication: for example, a magazine with comparatively few pages may be best suited to stapling, where staples go through each page of the magazine, including the cover, to hold the lot together. A magazine with several hundred pages, however, will require perfect binding (where individually folded sections are glued together to the inside of the cover, resulting in the flat spine common to most consumer magazines). A magazine with high production values and a high unit cost may even be hand-stitched rather than glued, rather like a hardback book, while in cases where the budget won't stretch to binding, the designer may opt to simply fold and hope for the best – the newspaper model.

Visionaire
Issue: 27
Design:
Design/Writing/
Research
USA

Spirale
Issue: 6/7 1958
Designer:
Camille Graeser
Switzerland

Flaunt
Issue: Feb 1998
Art directors:
Eric Roinestad
Jim Turner
Gerome Vizmanos
USA

TypoGraphic News
Issue: 77, 1996
Art directors:
Ian Styles
Becky Milner
David Quay
UK

Magazines are printed and bound in sections, and the economics of magazine production may well determine the shape and size of a magazine as well as the method by which it is bound: choosing a large format, for example, may mean that the printing must be done on a special press, and the binding by a special binder. When deviating from the norm, collaboration with a specialist magazine printer at an early stage allows the designer to find a size, shape, thickness and binding type that work well together, and are affordable.

karl seemann

spiel des dunkels
spiel der schatten
spiel des lichts

grundierung nacht

spiel-licht

der

schatten

konvois der schatten
konfiguration des lichts

filigrangeäst deines auges
gestreifter netzhaut
filigrangeäst deines auges
gestreifter netzhaut
filigrangeäst deines auges
gestreifter netzhaut

blau
blau
blau

stein
stein
stein

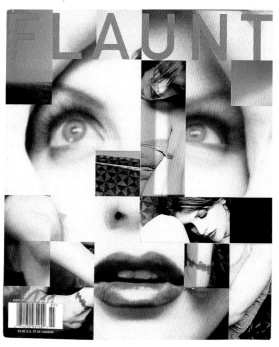

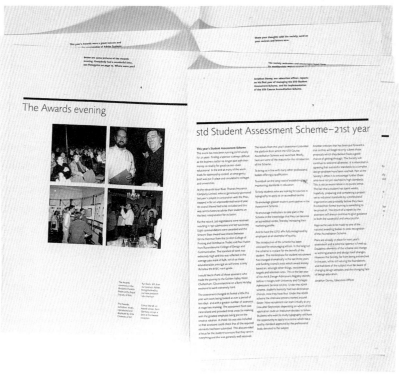

Bellybands

Bellybands have a variety of uses: first and foremost, they have a functional role, either discouraging people from leafing through the magazine before buying it, or allowing the publisher to attach a supplement or advertising inserts in the magazine without them becoming detached before purchase. The UK-based typographic magazine *Baseline* comes wrapped in a bellyband for a less practical reason: it is a stylistic device, allowing the actual cover of the magazine to remain free of words. The growth of sales in the American market, however, has now necessitated the printing of the magazine's details on the cover; other reasons for wrapping a magazine in a bellyband include the possibility of selling advertising space on the front of the magazine, without actually carrying advertising on the cover, and obscuring words or images that might cause offence or break the law. The bellyband buttoned across the front of *Nest* fulfils this role, as well as suggesting to readers the content of the magazine: it is concerned with homes and interiors. Readers might also infer from the use of fabric and the finish of a fully functional button that the magazine was in a league above its competitors in terms of price, and by extension quality. The first supposition is confirmed as soon as they pick it up; the second must wait until after they have wrestled with the button.

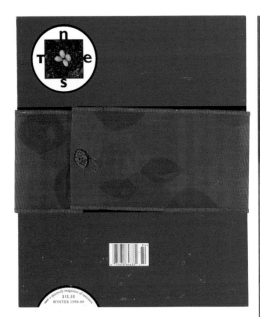

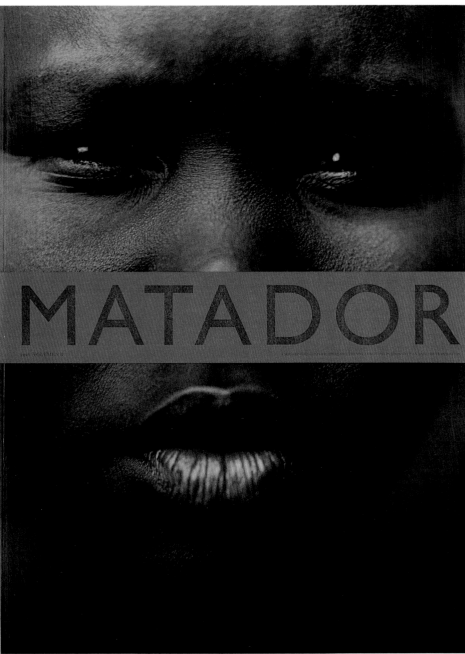

Nest
Issue: Winter 1998
Art director:
Joseph Holtzman
USA

Matador
Issue: 2 (B)
Art director:
Fernando Gutiérrez
Spain

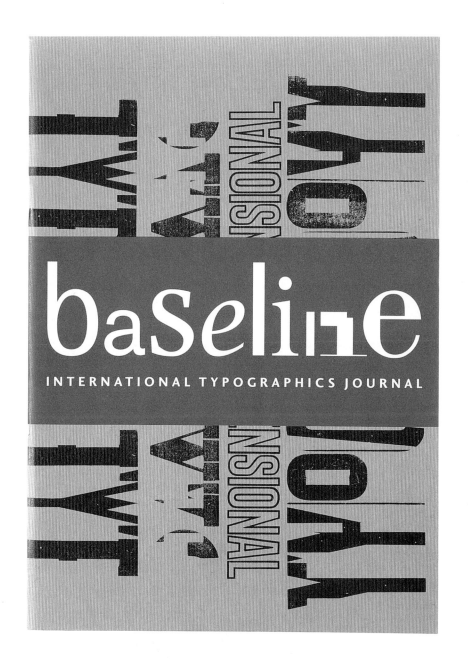

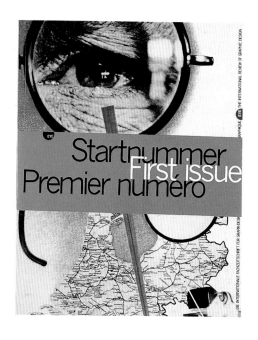

Baseline
Issue: 22, 1996
Art director:
hdr Design
UK

Eye
Issue: 1, 1990
Art director:
Stephen Coates
UK

'Binding' magazines in a box is impractical for large circulation publications as the finishing must be done by hand, making it a costly and time-consuming process. However, several small circulation or highly priced magazines have made a 'trademark' feature of this type of binding: The German magazine *Shift!*, for example, varies in format with every issue. It has variously been perfect bound, ringbound, hung on a butcher's hook and tied with string. The issue shown here, produced in association with the German Forum Typographie, is 'bound' in a plastic box, and takes the form of a series of menu cards. Another, incidental aspect of its design is that Helvetica is the only typeface used throughout. Similarly, The New York-

based fashion magazine *Visionaire* is produced in a box-bound format, as is the London-based fashion magazine *It*. In these cases, the unusual binding acts as an incentive to customers to pay the high prices these magazines command.

While many magazines are disposable, some are designed to be kept, and many such magazines give their readers means of protecting and organising their collections, such as branded binders or specially produced boxes (a free binder with the first issue is a common marketing tactic, designed to encourage the purchase of all issues thereafter). In other instances, boxes are produced as an afterthought: the typographic

magazine *Octavo*, for example, only ran for eight
issues, and a boxed set, designed for collectors, is
therefore not too cumbersome and allows the eight
magazines to be stored and examined as a complete
whole.

Boxes and bags are also often used to protect
magazines either on the shelf or in the mail. Some
designers have made a virtue of this fact, printing
a design on the protective sleeve itself, or creating
packaging whose construction makes the unwrapping
of the product an enticing prospect.

Creative Review
Issue: May 1999
Art director:
Nathan Gale
UK

dFusion
Issue: 1, 1998
Art director:
Stuktur Design
UK

Blueprint
Issue: May 1997
Art director:
Andrew Johnson
UK

Shift!
Issue: Power Games
Art director:
Anja Lutz
Germany

Octavo
Issue: 1–8
Art director:
8vo
UK

Format

**Interview
with Fernando Gutiérrez**

It was while studying graphic design at the London College of Printing that Fernando Gutiérrez first became fascinated by magazine design. It was in the early 1980s, and he now recalls eagerly awaiting the publication every month of *The Face*, just to see what its art director Neville Brody would do next. Gutiérrez himself experimented with magazine design at college, working on an avant-garde menswear title, and upon graduation, went to work for a variety of London design companies. At the first, he came into contact with Willy Fleckhaus' *Twen*, by then a good 20 years old, but a revelation nonetheless. His next posting, at CDT, brought him into the world of commercial publishing for the first time. Working under partner and editorial design expert Mike Dempsey, Gutiérrez was able to work on *Scene*, a lifestyle magazine that, unfortunately, never saw the light of day. It did, however, introduce him to a new way of looking at images and working with photographs, and it was an experience that remained with him when he moved to Spain in 1993. Gutiérrez himself was born in London to Spanish parents, and was attracted to the country by the dynamic changes that have occurred there since the end of Franco's rule in 1975, as well as the more traditional charms of a Mediterranean city such as Barcelona.

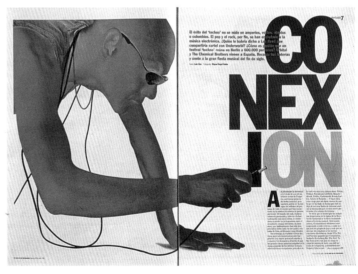

Gutiérrez's first job in Spain was with the Government's Institute for Youth, for which he designed a new magazine, *Injuve*. With an unusual large square format, and based on a double grid, the magazine was a hit, and lead to his second job – the design and art direction of *Tentaciones*, a newspaper supplement. The national daily *El País* was breaking new ground in Spain when in 1993 it commissioned a colourful supplement, designed to appeal to youth, to run in the otherwise austere-looking newspaper on Fridays. Gutiérrez landed the job, and the 48-page supplement proved to be enormously successful – so much so that the double page spreads that were a feature of the early issues were soon sacrificed to advertising.

Its distinctive covers, however, remained. Each is comprised of a brightly coloured icon, set in white space. The framework was decided partly by aesthetic considerations, and partly by practical ones: Gutiérrez was concerned that *Tentaciones* should look like a proper magazine, and as newspaper printing presses do not allow for full bleed printing, he elected to make the covers predominantly white anyway, to give the appearance of a full bleed. The masthead moves around the page in relation to the image – a freedom given by the fact that the magazine comes within a newspaper.

It was *Tentaciones* that attracted the attention of Tibor Kalman, then editor-in-chief of *Colors* magazine, who invited Gutiérrez to join the magazine in Rome as its art director. The invitation was initially turned down by Gutiérrez, for whom the effort of producing a 48-page magazine on a weekly basis had proved exhausting. As he notes now, magazine work has a tendency to take over a life, crowding out all other activities, including sleep: 'Working on magazines focuses you in a really obsessive way – it affects the way you see things – and it's really addictive.' But when Kalman called again six months later, Gutiérrez was ready to go, and spent the next two months of 1995 in Rome, art directing the famous issue 13 of *Colors* – the issue without words.

Immediately upon his return to Spain, another challenge presented itself, one that occupies him still, and will continue to demand attention until his sixtieth birthday, in the year 2022. Together with a former *El País* colleague, editor Alberto Anaut, and a printer, Titto Ferreira, Gutiérrez founded *Matador*, a yearly magazine about the times in which we live, with a special interest in culture and the arts.

Matador is, in many ways, unique: the infrequency with which it is published, and the six months each issue spends in production mean that it could never support full-time staff, or even make a decent profit – especially given that only 3,000 copies are ever printed. Its production is a labour of love on the part of its publishers, who decided from the outset that they would produce one issue for every letter of the Spanish alphabet – the 26 it shares with English plus 'ch', 'll' and 'ñ'. Its editors, designers, writers and photographers would use the magazine as a forum to discuss the times in which we live. The cast of contributors is distinguished and international (Henri Cartier-Bresson is one of the photographers), but the magazine would have a distinctively Spanish skew, and would be written in Spanish.

This emphasis on Spanishness, and on forgoing a new Spanish identity not just for design but for magazines as a whole, runs through Gutiérrez's work. As a Spanish designer who has not only lived and worked abroad, but worked on one of the world's truly international publications (*Colors*) he has unique insight into the matter. And for Gutiérrez, creating a local 'voice' for editorial design does not mean shutting out all outside influences: in *Matador*, for example, he uses a different typeface for each issue, 'resurrecting' some of the older faces with the intention of pointing out that they can still be beautiful. But the ones he has used so far – Gill Sans (issue one), Caslon 540 (issue two) News Gothic (issue three) Grotesk 9 (issue four) – are more closely associated with other countries. No, the distinctively Spanish qualities of Gutiérrez's work are more subtle, and more meaningful.

Each issue of *Matador* has a theme, and it is through the visual interpretation of it that Gutiérrez adds his contribution to the magazine's debate on what Spain and 'Spanishness' means. Issue two, for example, was 'Mediterranean'. Eschewing clichéd images of paradise beaches or olive groves, Gutiérrez instead opted to put the face of a then unknown African model, Alek Wek, on the cover. The image had particular resonance in Spain: due to its geographical location, the Mediterranean for Spain could be seen to represent the bridge between rich and poor, between the continents of Europe and Africa. Furthermore,

the African occupation of Spain in the time of the Moors has left permanent traces in the culture of modern Spain, as well as many historic buildings such as the Alhambra in Granada. While at first glance, the image may seem an odd choice for the cover of a magazine on the Mediterranean, its layers of meaning are numerous and profound. 'I don't like to do things just for the sake of doing them, to make a quick impression,' explains Gutiérrez. An ill-considered image can rebound on the credibility of the publication: 'You have to be constant, especially in magazines.' Does the position of art director carry with it a heavy responsibility in a content such as this, where a magazine participates in discussions on a topic as sensitive as national identity? 'Very much so,' he concurs, 'but I just want to make people think.'

The third issue of *Matador* was devoted to finding a new name and identity for Spain, which is made up of several autonomous and culturally distinct regions. As art director, Gutiérrez worked with writers and photographers to explain how they felt about living on the Iberian peninsula, in Spain and Portugal. The cover image is of a bone, part of a skeleton found recently. The idea behind it is that when that man was walking around the familiar landscape of Northern Spain 780,000 years ago, that not only was Spain not called Spain, but there were no regional or national borders, or cultural differences. Implicitly, it puts the debate into perspective.

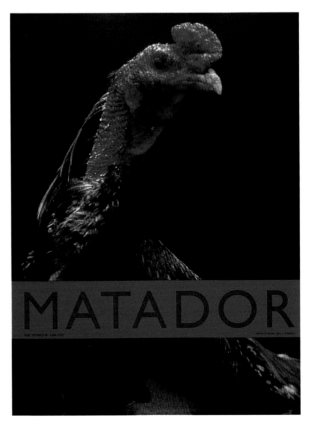

**Spread from
Matador 'A'
1995**

**Cover of
Matador 'CH'
1998**

**Cover of
Vanidad
Apr 1999**

**Cover of
Vanidad
Oct 1998**

**Cover of
Vanidad
Feb 1999**

**Spread from
Matador 'A'
1995**

The cover of issue four made no political points. The issue was guest-edited by the pop artist Eduardo Arroya and deals with his artistic influences. It contains material as diverse as Weegee's photographs of New York crime scenes and some reportage shots of a performance of Don Juan, with set design by Salvador Dalí. One of Arroya's passions is boxing, and he acts as a mentor to a heavyweight Hungarian fighter based in Germany. But instead of putting a boxer on the cover, Gutiérrez tried to find an image of a Cuban fighting rooster, washed down with rum. In the end, he settled for a Brazilian fowl, but the concept, and with it, a distinctively Hispanic flavour, remain.

Since 1998, Gutiérrez has also been art directing a Madrid-based fashion magazine, *Vanidad* (vanity). It had previously had 'a very baroque, Almodóvar image,' explains Gutiérrez, and he was called in by the publishers when they decided to revamp the magazine for launch in the Americas (where it is known as *Van*). They had observed that the needs and interests of the 300 million Spanish speakers in 19 South American countries, and the 20 million within the US, were not being met by the English language fashion press. Gutiérrez's response was to strip the magazine down to its bare essentials, aiming for an 'honest' approach. Dismissing the 'superficiality' of much of the fashion press, Gutiérrez explains that he 'thought *Vanidad* should create their own identity, and not comment so much on what other people were doing.' He kept the type as simple as possible –

'when you're driving, you don't worry about the gearbox: it should just work on its own' – and instead let the photographs do the talking. Navigation systems and other 'peripheral' information (page numbers, issue date and so on) are clearly and simply rendered. The overall impression is of a magazine confident of its perspective, and its culture, without being larded with 'symbolic' iconography – the bulls and fans approach.

The magazines designed by Fernando Gutiérrez – from *Tentaciones* to *Matador* and *Vanidad* – do not seek to be completely different from magazines produced either outside or within Spain. Increasingly, magazines are part of a global network where information and cultures are shared, and influence practices in other, far off places. But Gutiérrez's editorial design does have a strong Spanish perspective, rooted in the culture in which it operates, and the interests of the readers it serves. Gutiérrez's work demonstrates that while a fashion magazine is always first and foremost about fashion, it is also about readers, allowed to identify with a subject through design.

Most magazines are of a similar size and shape because they have to be: they may be distributed through the mail, or sell on the news-stand – both of which are made easier if the magazine is a conventional size. Specialist magazine printers are also set up to cope with magazines of a standard size. Deviate too far from the norm, and the print bill rises dramatically. The standard A4 portrait format also has design advantages: it is big enough to fit a reasonable amount of words and pictures on each page, while small enough to make for a manageable read.

Despite these considerations, some art directors feel that the advantages of producing an unusually-sized magazine outweigh the disadvantages. When seen against a back-drop of conventionally-sized publications, the uniquely-sized title stands out, which may give a fledgling 'alternative' publication the edge it needs to survive and succeed. A magazine with a smaller-than-average format might be reminiscent of a book, with the concomitant associations of permanence, collectability and substance. A larger-than-usual format gives the designer more space to play with – useful if the magazine makes a feature, for example, of highly detailed, good quality photography.

Tank
Issue: 3, Feb 1999
Art director:
Andreas Laeufer
Format: 180x150 mm
UK

What this micro-sized fashion magazine lacks in height and width, it makes up for in depth.

The Manipulator
Issue: 25, 1992
Editors:
Wilhelm Moser
and David Colby
Format: 700x500 mm
UK

Possibly the world's biggest magazine – *The Manipulator*'s enormous size means that it can only be read when it is rested on a (large) flat surface. Its size also makes it the perfect forum for showing off design work - its *raison d'être*.

THE MANIPULAT R

Iman.   photograph: Greg Gorman

ISSN 0178-3556   THE MANIPULATOR ISSUE NUMBER TWENTY-FIVE 1992   DM 18 FF 70 BFRS 490 £ 6 HFL 20 SFR 20 LIRE 18000 SEK 85 ÖS 150 CAN $15 U.S. $ 12

Big
Issue: 22
Art director:
Markus Kiersztan
Format: 305x240 mm
USA

The name of *Big* magazine is neatly reflected in its generous size.

Ampersand
Issue: 4, 1999
Art director:
Vince Frost
Format: 420x300 mm
UK

The large size of this house magazine for the British Design and Art Direction (D&AD) organisation allows for some lavish layouts, and D&AD's reputation rests on its ability to spot and promote good design.

Sleazenation
Issue: Jun 1998
Art director:
Guerilla6
Format: 250x200 mm
UK

The heavy paper stock and perfect-bound cover of this diminutive lifestyle publication give it a sense of substance.

AMPERSAND 4 NOMINATIONS ISSUE APRIL/MAY 1999 BRITISH DESIGN & ART DIRECTION

SLEAZE NATION

WORLD CUP BABYLON
TOSH + VIAGRA + KRONENBOURG +
SOUTHPORT SOUL WEEKENDER +
BARRY ADAMSON + BOUDICCA + BOWLING GREEN + FUEL

SN £2 JUNE '98

Spirale
Issue: 6/7, 1958
Cover design:
Marcel Wyss
Format: 350x350mm
Switzerland

Issue
Issue: 8
Art director:
Cartlidge Levene
Format: 420x297mm
UK

Interview
with Simon Esterson
Contents pages
Credits
Editorials
Navigation techniques
Dividers
Section changes
Standfirsts

Navigation

**Interview
with Simon Esterson**

Simon Esterson, along with his partner Mike Lackersteen, runs the highly successful and influential editorial design consultancy Esterson Lackersteen. Prior to founding the company, both partners had experience as magazine art directors – Esterson at the design and architecture journal *Blueprint* and Lackersteen as art director at contract publisher Redwood Publishing. In 1988, however, they decided to set up an independent studio specialising in editorial design.

It was a novel idea, as Esterson explains: 'At that time there were very few people within design companies that did editorial design. I did quite a lot of things at the same time as I was doing *Blueprint*, because people would always ring me up and say, could you look at our newspaper or magazine, and you'd end up doing it at the metaphorical kitchen table at midnight. And that didn't seem like a very good system. It seemed to me that having a proper studio to do those kind of things from was a good idea.'

Spread from
Sight and Sound
Jun 1997

Cover of
Sight and Sound
Mar 1998

Spread from
Sight and Sound
Oct 1998

Spread from
Sight and Sound
Aug 1998

The two designers had spotted a gap in the market: while most magazines have a full-time art director – a set-up Esterson describes as 'the best way to do magazines' – there were many others which, either because they published infrequently, or because budgets were small, found it difficult to justify employing an expensive professional full-time. The solution might have been to approach an independent design company, but as Esterson observes, 'The difference [between Esterson Lackersteen and other design companies] was that design groups didn't understand editorial design, and also that there was a difference in what design groups charged their corporate clients and what magazines were prepared to pay.' So Esterson Lackersteen was founded to cater for two core markets: the growing number of magazines which did not require the services of a full-time art director, and magazines wanting an outsider's perspective for a one-off redesign – a designer who could set up templates and style sheets before handing the day-to-day design of the magazine over to in-house designers.

'Of all the magazines produced, we miss out on the big bit in the middle,' explains Esterson, 'so the magazines we do every issue tend to be small magazines that can't afford their own art departments, like *Crafts*, the Royal Academy magazine and *Sight and Sound*. The other thing we do is design and re-design magazines for people, but that tends to be that group of trade magazines where there are fewer and fewer designers and more and more sub-editors, and what they want is a system that is a kit of parts, which they can move around in accordance with the demands of the content.'

For Esterson, though, the fact that his company art directs a number of magazines for several publishers on a regular basis does not mean that the designers cannot or should not be as intimately involved as a full-time, in-house art director might be: 'Although we're not physically in the office, the only reason to do them is to be absolutely involved with the subject matter. One publishing house has a system where it doesn't have in-house art directors, and just puts things on a bike to the designers at the end of the month. The danger there is that you're just going to get robot design. With *Sight and Sound*, the fact that the editor wasn't in the room didn't mean that I didn't read everything and discuss everything. He would often come to the studio, certainly during the production period.' Esterson places great importance on the relationships developed between the various parties working on a magazine, whether they work for the same company or not: 'I have been very fortunate in *Sight and Sound* and other magazines to have worked with editors whom one gets on with. And I know what [the editor] thinks about material, and I don't have to be in the room for him to know how I'll respond to something. Fundamentally, good magazines start with good editorial ideas, and then they have a team of people that are in sympathy with producing them, and can make those ideas work. It doesn't matter if it's four people in different parts of the world or in the same room.'

The same principle – of discussion and intimate engagement – applies equally to the magazines which the studio designs or redesigns and then hands over to an in-house team of designers. However, the fact that the studio will have no on-going involvement with the magazine after handing over the templates does affect the way the designers approach their task: 'If you get people in from outside, they have a certain objectivity about the process, and transfer ideas across titles. The danger of in-house design departments, particularly on trade titles, is that they get locked into a particular way of thinking and get more and more refined, until you get "the approach", which in the end becomes quite tired. What publishers want from you in those situations is a system that everybody can handle.' The outside art director must be sympathetic to the real needs of the magazine, and conscious of how the team will work to put the magazine together in their absence. In many instances, particularly with news weeklies, in-house magazines and the like, there may be no art editor, and the pages will be laid out by those whose primary skills lie elsewhere – reporters, sub-editors or production managers. And as Esterson says, where there is an art editor in residence, the case for sensitivity is even greater: 'If I were an art editor I wouldn't want a magazine that's just appeared from nowhere, so we like to talk with the designers about them. With the team as a whole, you want to feel that you're producing a magazine that they are happy with; that they understand the principle of it and can then apply it.'

Esterson suggests that for magazine publishers to use an outside designer instead of an in-house art department does not mean they have settled for second best; factors such as economies of scale mean that the client magazine receives a level of service not even many large, well-established magazines could afford in-house. Aside from the breadth of experience Esterson Lackersteen's designers have in magazine design. 'We can have more Macs and equipment working here for *Sight and Sound* than they could afford to have in their office.'

Each of the magazines designed by Esterson Lackersteen has its own dedicated designer within the company, who may well design more than one magazine. The two partners act as overseers on those magazines they do not actually design themselves. Although Esterson professes to have no intention of growing the studio to gargantuan proportions, it is already of a size where he and Lackersteen cannot exercise direct control over every aspect of the designs that come out of the studio. For a designer who feels too proprietorial about their own work, this could present a problem, but Esterson claims to cope well with such feelings: 'Ultimately, if you want to control everything you do, you work by yourself. I quite like collaboration – I think it's quite fun.'

Handing a cherished design over to a set of in-house designers, thereby surrendering all control over how it will be implemented, can present similar problems: 'It is very difficult,' acknowledges Esterson, 'because the strange thing about magazines is that they are terribly organic. I've been in a love/hate relationship with every magazine I've ever been involved with. There are magazines that I designed a long time ago and I still pick them up on the news-stand and am overjoyed that some things are still there and disappointed that other things have disappeared or are done badly.'

One of Esterson's main responsibilities today is as art director of *The Guardian* newspaper, where again he has to reconcile himself to the fact that he cannot control every layout or picture selection. And again he is philosophical: 'Not even someone who worked full time could have an overview of the paper every day. An editor has a struggle. So you rely on this team of people who are your delegates and your deputies who you trust and who can make it happen; and you need a really strict, direct chain of command.'

The life of the freelance art director is perhaps not for the control freak: time and financial constraints mean that however much the designer cares about an individual magazine, it is only ever a part-time job, and other projects must also be attended to. But as a way of working, it has its rewards, not least among which are creative freedom, variety, and the chance to experiment in a greater number of areas than would otherwise be possible: As Esterson puts it 'We're interested in being able to influence magazines and newspapers. And because you're objective, perhaps you can say "No" to something, or "Why don't you try this".' And rather than worry about the things he can't control, Esterson is happy enough to move on to the next challenge: 'I tend to be around when things start,' he enthuses, 'and then once they're up and running, after a few issues, I can drift off into something else.'

The catacomb-like heaps of bones exhumed from Cambodia's killing fields are a familiar, if grisly sight, but they are victims without faces. Less well-known are the prisoners of 'S-21' photographed by the Khmer Rouge

For such a small part of the magazine, the contents page has to work very hard. Although, as the name suggests, its primary function is to let the reader know what is in the magazine, and where it comes in the running order, it must do several other jobs on top of this: a section sometimes referred to as the 'flannel panel' (also sometimes known as the masthead) gives the names and job titles of everyone who works on the magazine, often with contact details as well. Many magazines also include background information about their contributors (*Arena*, *Graphics International*), or small foretastes of what each experienced in preparing their contribution. *Wallpaper*, for example, is ostensibly a magazine about interiors and design, but in reality this is just a vehicle for content about a general level of style and glamour most of its readers can only dream of. *Wallpaper*'s contents page plays up to this by including descriptions of the exciting places and exotic people encountered by its contributors in the process of compiling the magazine.

The editor's column may well sit on the page, along with details of circulation figures, subscription information and a publisher's disclaimer, denying responsibility for individual contributors' opinions or loss of submitted material. With all that information, an image or two is often inserted just to brighten the view. It's the designer's job to get all of that complex, heterogeneous information on to one, or perhaps two pages, while still allowing the reader to discover what they want to know – who is the advertising sales manager, what page does the main interview start on – at a glance. No mean feat.

The arrangement and presentation of information on the contents page should reflect the nature of the material that is to follow: for instance, if a news section is followed by a clearly defined features section, the two should be identified as distinct through devices such as a change of colour or typeface on the contents page. *Arena* is arranged in sections dealing with news, fashion, reviews and so on, and the contents page

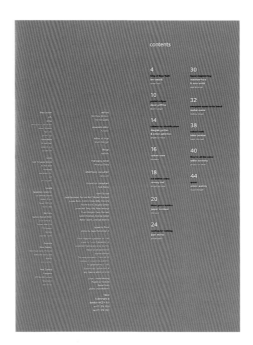

Frieze
Issue: 2, 1991
Art director:
Nashville
UK

Dazed & Confused
Issue: Aug 1997
Art director:
Matt Roach
UK

Graphics
International
Issue: Feb 1996
Art director:
MetaDesign
UK

The Sunday Times
Issue: May 1998
Art director:
Andrew McConachie
UK

follows this pattern. Although the features are listed in the order in which they appear in the magazine, they are broken up by headings in large type, identifying the section in which they can be found. Within the body of the magazine, these sections are made distinct from one another through the use of design.

The examples shown here demonstrate the range of ways in which art directors have been able to present very similar information: in some cases functionality is of paramount importance to the designer, in other cases an appealing appearance is a greater priority. In all cases, however, a fine balance has been struck. Functionality was the key consideration in the design of *Graphics International*'s contents page, and a rigid typographic hierarchy allows the reader to access the information they want quickly and easily; for example, contributors' names, arranged alphabetically, are highlighted in bold, with their biographies in plain text. The contents themselves are arranged in a continuous list, with the special report highlighted by means of a keyline box.

The framework remains the same from issue to issue, compounding the sense that the primary function of the page is to provide information as efficiently as possible. The modern art magazine *Frieze*, on the other hand, changes the style of its contents page with each issue, introducing a sense of experimentation into the magazine early on. Likewise, in his own words, Vince Frost 'had a lot of fun' with the contents pages of *Big*. Each of the ten issues he designed were different, and took experimentation to its limits. Even so, the pages are surprisingly navigable. Similarly, while there is a logic to the typographic styling of *Dazed & Confused*'s contents page, an arresting and entertaining appearance was of paramount importance for this style magazine.

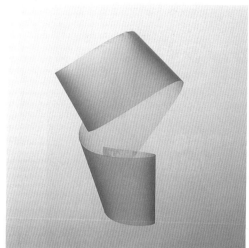

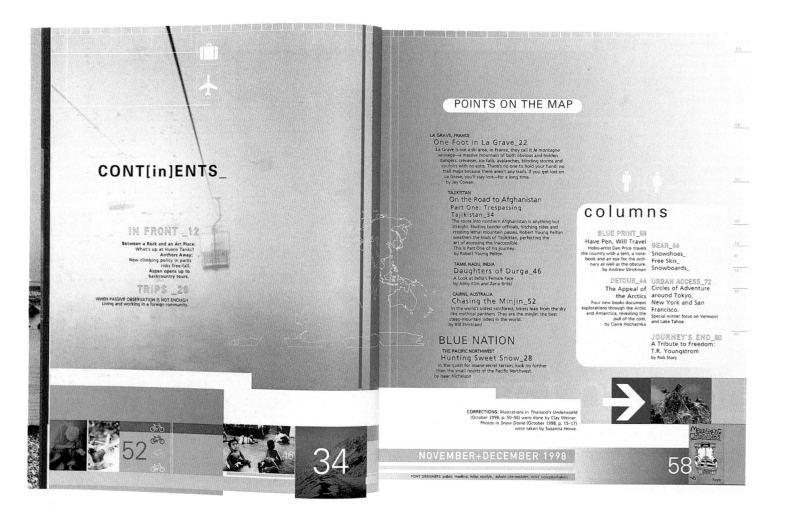

CONT[in]ENTS_

IN FRONT _12

Between a Rock and an Art Place:
What's up at Hueco Tanks?
Anchors Away:
New climbing policy in parks
risks free-fall.
Aspen opens up to
backcountry tours.

TRIPS _20

WHEN PASSIVE OBSERVATION IS NOT ENOUGH
Living and working in a foreign community.

POINTS ON THE MAP

LA GRAVE, FRANCE
One Foot in La Grave_22
La Grave is not a ski area. In France, they call it *le montagne sauvage*—a massive mountain of both obvious and hidden dangers: crevasses, ice falls, avalanches, blinding storms and couloirs with no exits. There's no one to hold your hand; no trail maps because there aren't any trails. If you get lost on La Grave, you'll stay lost—for a long time.
by Jay Cowan

TAJIKISTAN
On the Road to Afghanistan
Part One: Trespassing
Tajikistan_34
The route into northern Afghanistan is anything but straight. Eluding border officials, hitching rides and crossing lethal mountain passes, Robert Young Pelton weathers the trials of Tajikistan, perfecting the art of accessing the inaccessible.
This is Part One of his journey.
by Robert Young Pelton

TAMIL NADU, INDIA
Daughters of Durga_46
A Look at India's Female Face
by Abby Ellin and Zana Briski

CAIRNS, AUSTRALIA
Chasing the Minjin_52
In the world's oldest rainforest, bikers leap from the sky like mythical panthers. They are the *minjin*: the best steep-mountain riders in the world.
by Bill Strickland

BLUE NATION

THE PACIFIC NORTHWEST
Hunting Sweet Snow_28
In the quest for insane secret terrain, look no further than the small resorts of the Pacific Northwest.
by Isaac Nichelson

columns

BLUE PRINT_58
Have Pen, Will Travel
Hobo-artist Dan Price travels the country with a tent, a notebook and an eye for the ordinary as well as the obscure.
by Andrew Strickman

GEAR_64
Snowshoes_
Free Skis_
Snowboards_

DETOUR_64
The Appeal of the Arctics
Four new books document explorations through the Arctic and Antarctica, revealing the pull of the cold.
by Claire Hochachka

URBAN ACCESS_72
Circles of Adventure around Tokyo, New York and San Francisco.
Special winter focus on Vermont and Lake Tahoe.

JOURNEY'S END_80
A Tribute to Freedom:
T.R. Youngstrom
by Rob Story

CORRECTIONS: Illustrations in *Thailand's Underworld* (October 1998, p. 50–56) were done by Clay Weiner. Photos in *Snow Dome* (October 1998, p. 15–17) were taken by Susanna Howe.

NOVEMBER+DECEMBER 1998

FONT DESIGNERS: pablo medina, miles newlyn, edwin utermohlen, newt wongsunkakon

Blue
Issue: Dec 1998
Art director:
Christa Skinner
Design consultant:
David Carson
USA

Sight and Sound
Issue: Jan 1997
Art director:
Simon Esterson
(Esterson
Lackersteen)
UK

Wallpaper
Issue: Sep/Oct 1996
Art director:
Herbert Winkler
UK

Sight and Sound
(incorporating Monthly
Film Bulletin)
Volume 7 Issue 1 (NS)
Editorial office:
21 Stephen Street
London W1P 1PL
Telephone 0171 255 1444
Facsimile 0171 436 2327
Email: S&S@bfi.org.uk
Subscription offers:
01858 435528

Editorial
Editor
Philip Dodd
Acting deputy editor
Nick James
Acting associate editor
Leslie Felperin
Associate editor
Ian Christie
Assistant editor
Colette O'Reilly
Credits research
Julian Grainger
Research assistant
William Neil
Contributing editors
J. Hoberman, Pervaiz Khan,
John Powers, Mike O'Pray, Tony
Rayns, Jane Root, Amy Taubin
Subeditor
Mark Sinker
Picture editor
Millie Simpson
Design and art direction
Esterson Lackersteen
Origination
Precise Litho
Printer
St Ives plc

Advertising sales
David Thomas
Telephone 0171 957 8916
Facsimile 0171 436 2327

Business
Publishing director
Caroline Moore
Publishing assistant
Nichola Roth
Managing director
BFI publishing
Colin MacCabe
Newsstand distribution
UMD. Telephone 0171 638 4666
Bookshop distribution
Central Books
Telephone 0181 986 4854
US distribution
Periodicals postage paid at
Rahway, NJ, and at additional
mailing offices. Postmaster:
send address corrections to
Sight and Sound, c/o Mercury
Airfreight International Ltd Inc.,
2323 Randolph Avenue,
Avenel, NJ 07001
Subscription price is $67.00
Newsstand distribution by:
Eastern News Distributors Inc.

Annual subscription rates
UK £31.50
Europe £38.50
US/Canada airspeed £38.50
Overseas surface mail £38.50
Overseas airmail £66.00
Special rates apply to BFI
members

Subscription queries
For subscription queries and sales
of back issues and binders contact
Subscription Department,
Sight and Sound
Tower House, Sovereign Park
Market Harborough
Leicestershire LE16 9EF
Telephone 01858 435528
Facsimile 01858 434958

The British Film Institute exists
to encourage the development
of film, television and video in the
United Kingdom, and to promote
knowledge, understanding and
enjoyment of the culture of the
moving image. Its activities
include the National Film and
Television Archive; the National
Film Theatre; the Museum of the
Moving Image; the London Film
Festival; the production and
distribution of film and video;
funding and support for regional
activities; Library and Information
Services; Stills, Posters and
Designs; Research; Publishing
and Education; and the monthly
Sight and Sound magazine

Published monthly by the
British Film Institute
ISSN 0037-4806

Sight and Sound

January 1997

Features

THE DEAD
From *The Deer Hunter* onwards,
Christopher Walken has been the
most compelling and cadaverous
of screen actors. By Ian Penman **6**

DESPERATION AND DESIRE
Nicolas Roeg's study of
bereavement, memory and the
occult, *Don't Look Now*, is also an
exquisite, icy time machine,
argues Leslie Dick **10**

THE LOOK OF 'EVITA'
What look has Alan Parker's
Evita invented for Eva Perón and
Argentina? The costume designer
and production designer explain.
Interviews by Stella Bruzzi and
Leslie Felperin **14**

ANDREI TARKOVSKY
On the tenth anniversary of his
death, *Sight and Sound* celebrates
the work of Andrei Tarkovsky
THE WEIGHT OF THE WORLD
Julian Graffy tours Tarkovsky's
elemental world **18**
NEVER BE NEUTRAL
Layla Alexander Garrett
remembers working with
Tarkovsky in exile **22**
SEEING IS BELIEVING
French director Olivier Assayas
discusses the visceral impact of
Tarkovsky's autobiographical film
Mirror with Bérénice Reynaud **24**
H FOR HITCHCOCK
From knives to lovely cool
torments. David Thomson
on Alfred Hitchcock **26**

Film Reviews

Acts of Love **34**
Daylight **35**
Feeling Minnesota **36**
Glimmer Man, The **37**
Island Of Dr. Moreau, The **38**
Jingle All the Way **39**
Last of the High Kings, The **40**
Loco de amor/Two Much **53**
Midsummer Night's Dream, A **41**
101 Dalmatians **42**
Roald Dahl's Matilda **43**
Robinson in Space **44**
Shine **44**
Sleepers **45**
Some Mother's Son **46**
Starmaker, The/
L'uomo delle stelle **47**
Star Trek First Contact **48**
Sunchaser, The **50**
Surviving Picasso **51**
Through the Olive Trees/
Zir-e darakhtan-e zeyton/
Under the Olive Trees **52**
Two Much/Loco de amor **53**
Under the Olive Trees/
Through the Olive Trees/
Zir-e darakhtan-e zeyton **52**
uomo delle stelle, L'/
The Starmaker **47**
Walking and Talking **54**
Zir-e darakhtan-e zeyton/
Through the Olive Trees/
Under the Olive Trees **52**

Video Reviews

Tom Tunney and Geoffrey Macnab
on this month's video releases **58**

**Next issue on sale
28 January**

Regulars

EDITORIAL Local villains **3**
BUSINESS Tarantino versus the
film unions; Cannes kerfuffle;
Branagh's *Hamlet* **4**
THE BOX News in the Future;
TV Chefs; *Brass Eye*; Soap news **31**
LETTERS *Underground*; G for Gags;
film studies **64**
COVER Christopher Walken
photographed by Gizard/Retna

Alfred Hitchcock: 26

'Shine': 44

'Star Trek First Contact': 48

Madonna in 'Evita': 14

---

contentsliving autumn

034 Clairtone and Electrohome: two companies that transformed
60s stereo design. *He wears suit and shirt from Club Monaco*

078 Wallpaper's answer to the modern bachelor pad

094 sampling
the new
Sunday lunch

Intelligence
019 The making of Miss Minimalism. Why fashionable
Manhattan is beating a path to Deborah Berke's door.
026 News: Manchester gets some Air; trams for Hanover;
bars for the girls.
028 Squire Boy. The correct way to shop.

Hot sheet
030 A library of ideas. Dutch architects Mecanoo are
masters of construction.
034 Sphere and Now. The sound in the round that put
Canada on the industrial design map.

Urban life
040 The uncomplicated commute. Why risk road rage?
Five slick ways to get around town.

Reportage
048 Neo Neighbourhood. Marcus Field looks into the
urban future and predicts the return of the village.

Media
058 News: Reviews of John Pawson's *Minimum* and *STUD
Architectures of Masculinity*. Plus a CD-ROM devoted to the
Austrians who modernised America.

Agenda
063 Important dates for your diary

Home office
065 Business studies. Creating a workable space. By Kate Taylor.

In house
069 Easy as ply. Michael Horsham heralds a new wave for plywood.
073 Forever Young. Furniture designer Michael Young
on why he's not retro.
074 News: In bed with Tocca; 100% design; the bean bag is back.

Features

The space
078 Life in a single space. Our stylists create the perfect
pad for a time pressed urbanite.

Dream pad
088 Palm Springs meets Penzance. Wallpaper's designs
for a tropical retreat - two hours from London.

The event
094 The new Sunday lunch. Round up your friends and
relax with food from three continents.

Food stuff
100 Essential autumn. Laura Ljungkvist draws out the
must haves for the well stocked kitchen.

The dish
108 Death of the two-hour lunch. Daisy Wakamatsu cooks
up portable meals to suit the new working day.

Short orders
117 Iceberg ahead. No longer a has-been, iceberg lettuce is
cool, crisp and back on the table. Plus three wines to try and
Nobu to the rescue.

160 Resources

wallpaper* | **009**

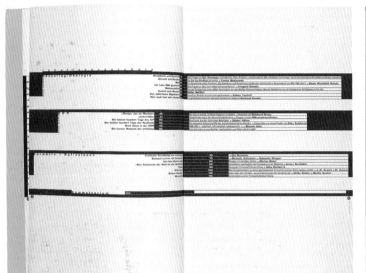

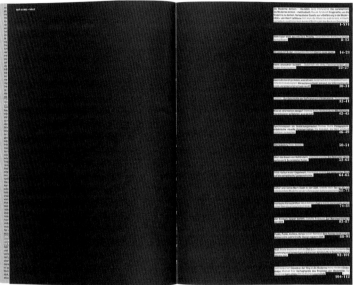

Form & Zweck
Issue: 2/3, 1991
Art director: cyan
Germany

Form & Zweck
Issue: 4/5, 1992
Art director: cyan
Germany

A Be Sea
Issue: Summer 1993
Produced by:
Bryan Maloney
and Sharon John
UK

sleazenation
Issue: Oct 1998
Art director:
Andrew Cunning
UK

Ray Gun
Issue: 38
Art director:
Robert Hales
USA

contents

レイカン

Raygun 0.38

Small Print

violent onsen geisha; sugar plant; guitar wolf; melt-banana; dmbq; giant robot

Buffalo Daughter

Super Deformed Gundams

Super Junky Monkey

Pugs

Uresei Yatsura

Japanimation

Cornelius

Shibuya Scene

Garage Girls

Yoko Ono + Cibo Matto

Big in Japan

beastie boys; radiohead; cheap trick; blur; ben folds five; the cardigans; jmascis

Boredoms

Electronica

dj krush; ryuichi sakamoto; ken ishii; haruomi hosono; tetsu inoue

Pizzicato Five + Towa Tei

Nanaco

Hysteric Glamour

Japanese Zines

It Bytes

Karl Taro Greenfeld

Yohji Yamamoto

Last Page

august 1996

contents

(Hot Space 1996...Let's Go!)

Big in **Japan** Issue

store my duck

sleazenation
volume.2.issue.x

08.10
Les Bruits Qui Courent

08.24
Unusual Suspects

08.26
Grant Morrison

08.28
Vincent Gallo

08.34
Andrew Groves

08.40
My Work is Directional

08.52
Smoking

08.64
Stylist with Chalk

08.73
Quickspace

08.74
Spleen

08.75
Kahuna Cuts

08.76
Dymasion

08.77
Estereo

08.78
Prozak Trax

08.80
Digital Hardcore Recordings

08.82
Volume All* Star

08.91
Savoir Vivre

Credits

As was described over the last few pages, contents pages almost always carry some information about the magazine's contributors - even if it is just their name (though some, such as *The Economist*, omit even that; its authority comes from its own brand name, and not from the identity of its writers). Often, biographical details or amusing anecdotes are added, either to increase the credibility of the writers - and consequently the magazine - in the eyes of the reader, or just to inject a sense of personality into the proceedings at an early stage.

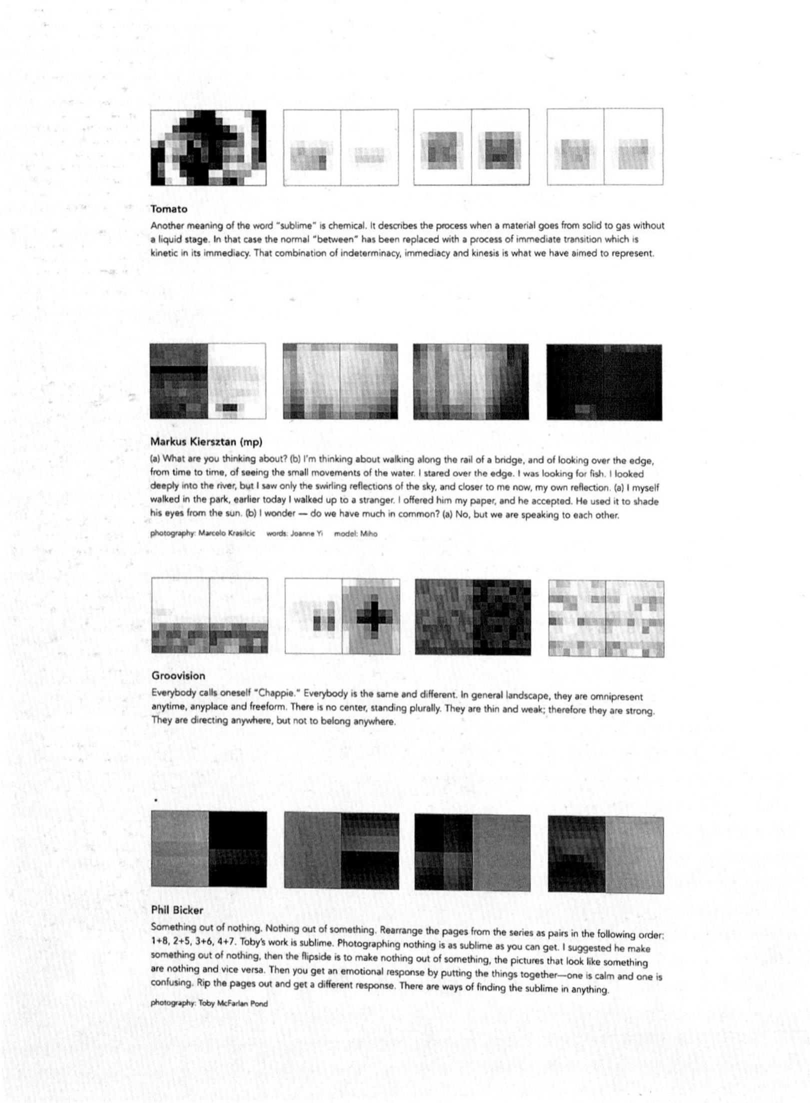

Tomato

Another meaning of the word "sublime" is chemical. It describes the process when a material goes from solid to gas without a liquid stage. In that case the normal "between" has been replaced with a process of immediate transition which is kinetic in its immediacy. That combination of indeterminacy, immediacy and kinesis is what we have aimed to represent.

Markus Kiersztan (mp)

(a) What are you thinking about? (b) I'm thinking about walking along the rail of a bridge, and of looking over the edge, from time to time, of seeing the small movements of the water. I stared over the edge. I was looking for fish. I looked deeply into the river, but I saw only the swirling reflections of the sky, and closer to me now, my own reflection. (a) I myself walked in the park, earlier today I walked up to a stranger. I offered him my paper, and he accepted. He used it to shade his eyes from the sun. (b) I wonder — do we have much in common? (a) No, but we are speaking to each other.

photography: Marcelo Krasilcic words: Joanne Yi model: Miho

Groovision

Everybody calls oneself "Chappie." Everybody is the same and different. In general landscape, they are omnipresent anytime, anyplace and freeform. There is no center, standing plurally. They are thin and weak; therefore they are strong. They are directing anywhere, but not to belong anywhere.

Phil Bicker

Something out of nothing. Nothing out of something. Rearrange the pages from the series as pairs in the following order: 1+8, 2+5, 3+6, 4+7. Toby's work is sublime. Photographing nothing is as sublime as you can get. I suggested he make something out of nothing, then the flipside is to make nothing out of something, the pictures that look like something are nothing and vice versa. Then you get an emotional response by putting the things together—one is calm and one is confusing. Rip the pages out and get a different response. There are ways of finding the sublime in anything.

photography: Toby McFarlan Pond

Philip Agee makes place-specific and limited-edition furniture, ceramics, and small sculptures in his studio/workshop in San Francisco. His partner, **Stephen Penkowsky,** is an exhibition-designer whose major interests are modern and Asian design. *Photos: Bill Clay*

Ed Frascino, who reads tarot cards, has published a collection of his *New Yorker* cartoons, *Avocado is Not Your Color (and Other Scenes of Married Bliss). Eddie Spaghetti*, his historical novel for nine-year-olds, was published some years ago. *Photo: Michelle Barclay*

Julia Alvarez is a poet, essayist, and fiction writer who spent her childhood in the Dominican Republic. She is the author of *How the Garcia Girls Lost their Accents, In the Time of the Butterflies, ¡Yo!, The Other Side,* and *Homecoming*. Her book of essays, *Something to Declare*, was published this fall. *Photo: Bill Eichner*

Jim Goldberg is a photographer, video-maker, and writer. He is best known for his books and exhibits, among them *Rich and Poor, Nursing Home, Hospice* and, most recently, *Raised by Wolves.* He has received numerous awards and grants including a Guggenheim Fellowship, three National Endowment for the Arts awards, and a Eureka Fellowship. *Photo: Jane Wattenberg*

Adam Bartos is the co-author of *International Territory: the United Nations 1945–1995* (with text by Christopher Hitchens). His work is represented in the permanent collections of the Houston Museum of Fine Arts and the New York MoMA. He is currently working on photographs taken in Russia.

Glen Helfand is a free-lance writer, curator, and former graphic designer. His writing on art, culture, and technology has appeared in *The Bay Guardian, Wired, Limn, Salon, Travel and Leisure, The Advocate, LA Weekly,* and the *San Francisco Examiner.*

Bernard Cooper is the author of *Maps to Anywhere* and *Truth Serum*. He is the recipient of the 1991 PEN/USA Ernest Hemingway Award. His work has appeared in several periodicals and anthologies, including *The Best American Essays of 1998, The Penguin Book of Gay Short Stories,* and *The Paris Review. Photo: Bonnie Schiffman*

Matthias Herrmann is a Vienna-based photographer with an unmistakable German accent. As Andrea Fitzpatrick correctly observes, "He's talented, he's hot, and he takes pictures of his penis." Although Herrmann's work has been shown extensively throughout Europe, he's making his nesr debut in this issue. *Photo: Matthias Herrmann*

Richard Davies lives in London and works as an architectural and interiors photographer. His clients include the architects Foster & Partners, Future Systems, David Chipperfield, and John Pawson.

Jack Hope, an outdoor writer, lives in Manhattan. He has written extensively about the wilderness of North America, and is the author of the books *Yukon* and *A River for the Living.*

John Divola is a photographer who lives in Venice, California. His work has been exhibited extensively worldwide, at Seibu Gallery, Tokyo; Camera Obscura, Stockholm; and Gallerie del Cavallino, Venice, Italy; as well as at numerous American galleries and museums. Mr. Divola teaches art at the University of California, Riverside.

Michael Huey was born in Michigan and studied German at Amherst College. In 1989 he moved to Vienna, where is currently a graduate student in art history. His thesis investigates the neo-rococo renovation of the Palais de Liechtenstein. Mr. Huey worked for *The Christian Science Monitor* and writes for *The World of Interiors.*

Simon Doonan, designer of the notorious window displays at Barneys New York, grew up fearing for his sanity among a horde of loony relatives. The essential elements of window display, improbable tableaux and wacky visual nonsequiturs, were part of his daily life and, he claims, informed his creative sensibility. *Photo: Justin Sutcliffe*

Kevin Killian is a poet, novelist, critic, and playwright. His books include *Bedrooms Have Windows, Shy, Little Men, Arctic Summer,* and *Argento Series.* With Lewis Ellingham he authored *Poet Be Like God: Jack Spicer and the San Francisco Renaissance* (Wesleyan, 1998), the first biography of this important American poet. *Photo: Craig Goodman*

Mitch Epstein is working on a photographic project about public and private life in Manhattan. His photos from *Vietnam: A Book of Changes* are currently on view at The Center for Documentary Studies in Durham, North Carolina.

The late **Paul László** was an unusual architect, interior, and industrial designer who leavened Bauhaus Modernism with color and ornament. Escaping the Nazis, László brought his luxurious clarity to Beverly Hills patrons, who unstintingly let László create houses complete with lighting, furnishing and accessories.

Big
Issue: 22
Publisher
and director:
Marcelo Jünemann
Creative director:
Markus Kiersztan
USA

Nest
Issue: Winter 1998
Art director:
Joseph Holtzman
USA

TypoGraphic
Issue: 52, 1998
Art director:
Nick Bell
UK

The editor's column, or editorial, usually sits on or near the contents page, and differs from the rest of the magazine's content in that it is a direct address by the editor to the reader - the equivalent of a newspaper's leader column, in which the editor is free to pronounce on the issues of the day, or any other subject that takes their fancy. They are often used for describing just how wonderful the rest of the magazine's content is. Although there is very little deviation between magazines as far as style goes - it is just a column of text after all - readers will subconsciously learn a lot about the tone of the magazine from the pieces of information that surround it: a photograph of the editor and a hand-written signature might signify a friendly, approachable tone, for example.

Few magazines stray very far outside the parameters of convention in their treatment of the editor's column; one exception is *Dazed & Confused*: the style magazine regularly includes bizarre and incongruous items in place of the editor's column, from a questionnaire, sent to the editor by a fan, to a mocked-up arrest record, noting various 'charges' laid against the editor, implicitly by his own staff.

01/6 RICK POYNOR: **What we have now, as each new rule-breaking, ground-shaking collection chases the tail of the last, is a new orthodoxy every bit as predictable and unimaginative as the old professional orthodoxy that the new graphic design sought to overturn.** 02/36 DAVID HEATHCOTE: **The themes of modularity, industrialisation and rationality are represented by minimal text and clear typography.** 03/64 HERBERT SPENCER (1967): **The frontiers between graphic design, photography, and typography have dissolved; the marriage of word and image has been consummated.** 04/40 STEVE HELLER: **In time, more magazine editors will accept the visual essay as an integral component of the editorial mix.** 05/5 JESSICA HELFAND: **Aesthetic innovation, if it exists at all, occurs within ridiculously preordained parameters: a new plug-in, a modified code, the capacity to make pictures and words "flash" with a mouse in a nonsensical little dance.** 06/26 ANNE BURDICK: **I predict a move away from the cacophony of typefaces towards a cleaner aesthetic. We kind of hit the Baroque phase of that a while back at CalArts.** 07/10 ADRIAN FRUTIGER: **I am sure in some years from now you will see new posters with just white space and four lines in Garamond.** 08/26 GAIL SWANLUND: **My students are extraordinarily conservative. I think maybe it's a reaction to all the technology.** 09/82 JAMES SOUTTAR: **Ideological Modernism, far from being consigned to the dustbin of history, is alive and well and living under an assumed name. Information design is engaged in a well-orchestrated struggle to dominate the moral high ground in graphic design – and is succeeding.** 10/81 PAUL RENNER: **The truly Modern, that is, the undistorted expression of an objective zeitgeist, is only what we hold today to be timelessly perfect. This is not the same in all periods, because the insight into the timelessly valid changes from generation to generation.** 11/40 STEVE HELLER: **For some illustrators the visual essay is a means to cover events, for others it is a door to uncover deeper meaning.** 12/36 MICHAEL WORTHINGTON: **The computer has really closed the gap between ideation and production. There's a more fluid process of sketching with the computer.**

Editorial

Modernism's programme of educating and elevating the masses to a better life is nowadays often ridiculed as the naïve idealism of a thoroughly bourgeois culture. In the end, the critics say, it didn't spark a revolution as much as it served to uphold the status quo by smoothing global capitalism's operations. The once highly moral project of Modern Life after World War II became an ideology of mere contemporaneity before dumbing down in the 1980s and 1990s to the hedonistic superficialities of an ever faster-moving cycle of *lifestyles*.[1]

Modernism, it may be recalled, at the beginning of this century made use of a combination of two, seemingly opposed, strategies for attaining its utopian goals: rationalisation and storytelling. On the one hand it promoted a rational approach to

SAMPLING organising information, to clarity and cleanliness, to a kind of design that through its openness and honesty, and its allergy to decorum, would provide the perfect communication tools for a true democracy.[2] On the other hand the Modernist avant-garde of the 1920s developed new ways of communicating "content" (be it art or advertising), that aimed at convincing their audience through aesthetic enhancements of the designs.[3] Collage, photomontage and the "photo-essay"[4] became powerful accessories to verbal argumentation and storytelling, to the extent that, before long, the visual style of a message was the argument. Modernism's rationalist tendencies reached their peak at the Ulm design school which closed in 1968, and it has since definitively exhausted itself in 1960s and 1970s corporate design and architecture, leaving a legacy of Spartan morals from which to design "essential" things. Or so it seems, from a postmodern perspective.

MODERN Modernism's other, "visual storytelling" strand lived longer. But gradually, the idealistic – and ideological – ties that bound form and content into one message loosened. In the end, the ethically connotated "machine aesthetic" of the 1920s became aesthetics. A style to be used to suggest modernity, rather than Modernism. The ethical imperative that was at the root of the "form follows function" idea still lingered in the layered aesthetics of "early postmodernism", where one could argue that complexities of style reflected newly realised complexities of technology and new insights in the multi-level character of messages. In this light, "deconstructivism" may be seen as a last attempt at making messages, complex as they are, "transparent". Of course, it resulted in being quite the contrary . . .[5] And then there was postmodernism. Now what?

Strangely enough, Modernism seems to be on the way back.[6] Adrian Frutiger, on his seventieth birthday last year, was celebrated not so much as a Last Mohican, but rather as a role model and a still powerful source of inspiration, and his typefaces adorn both airport time schedules and house party flyers.[7] The difference is that the recent and hip recyclings of Modernist forms and formats do without the once obligatory reference to a style that would "truly" match the "machine aesthetics" of a technological world. If form follows anything these days, it is targets. More likely, it seems that the resurgent interest in Modernism's aesthetic gamut indicates a feeling of exhaustion

THE after the visual abundance of the past decade,[8] rather than a need for "rational" and "honest" forms. Remnants of the Ulm legacy, however, are revived in booming disciplines such as interface and information design,[9] where they serve to get a hold on the ever growing complexities of ever more intricately mixed messages and media.

The recent re-assessment of Modernist aesthetics, thus, frequently shows a lack of understanding for the project that Modernism once was – or a disappointed refusal to think in the all-encompassing terms associated with the old ideology.[10] "Visual storytelling" is alive and well, increasingly understood as a way to reflect in depth on current affairs as well as the state of the cultural discourse.[11] But although the forms and formats of Modernist visual languages are well established, the imperative of matching form, content and intention that inspired it, is all but forgotten. The computer may have short-circuited thinking and doing in design,[12] but all too often in the rapid transition from idea to product the argumentation that should ideally ground the one on to the other is weakened. In a large number of today's information design products, Modernist narrativity is reduced to its prosaic fundamentals, disregarding the poetics of seduction that was originally such an inspiration. Re-assessment of Modernism would mean looking at the whole picture, instead of sampling only the bits from the heritage that match one's practical or ideological preferences. Kandinsky summarised the need to overcome the either-ors of stylistic and

INHERITANCE methodological orthodoxy quite poignantly in his plea for inclusiveness in the arts and design: "UND." Re-marrying poetry to structure, argumentation to point of view, thinking to acting, ideal to practice, seems to be a sensible agenda in our age of integration of technologies, disciplines and discourses.

EYE 31/99 3

Eye
Issue: 31, 1999
Art director:
Nick Bell
UK

Dazed & Confused
Issue: 34, 1997
Art director:
Molson Deckard
UK

Emigre
Issue: 19, 1991
Art director:
Rudy Vanderlans
USA

Graceland

June 21, 1997

Mr. Jefferson Hack
Dazed & Confused
112-116 Old Street
London
ENGLAND
EC1V 9BD

Dear Mr. Hack:

Your letter of 20 May to Elvis Presley was forwarded to me for reply. As Mr. Presley has been deceased for some twenty years, he is presently unavailable for an interview. However, your comments regarding his stature as a role model and cultural icon, and your interest in featuring his image on the cover of your first issue of the year 2000, are greatly appreciated. We do not anticipate any change in the status of Mr. Presley's availability for an interview, but we should be in a position to provide you with updated information about his never-ending career and possibly a good photograph for your cover. When the time comes, please get back in touch.

Rumors regarding Mr. Presley's comeback as the new millennium approaches are not entirely without merit. On 16 August of this year, Mr. Presley, via video technology, will "perform" in a historic live entertainment event. "Elvis in Concert '97", staged at the Mid-South Coliseum in Memphis, will bring together the Memphis Symphony Orchestra and over thirty of Elvis' original former bandmates to perform live, with Elvis himself singing lead vocal. Among the band members will be J.D. Sumner & The Stamps, The Jordanaires, The Sweet Inspirations, The Imperials, Voice, The TCB Band, Scotty Moore, D.J. Fontana, and others. It is possible that a similar production, cast list and overall production scaled to road show size, could tour the world within a couple of years.

Your coverage of "Elvis in Concert '97", along with all of the events in Memphis that are part of Elvis Week this year, is invited. For press credentials and further information you can contact our publicity agent, David Beckwith, in Los Angeles at 213-845-9836 or Fax 213-845-9023.

Thank you very much for your interest in working with Elvis Presley and for the copy of your impressive magazine.

Sincerely,

Todd Morgan
Director of Creative Resources
Graceland/Elvis Presley Enterprises, Inc.

ST. JAMES'S PALACE
LONDON SW1A 1BS

From: The Press Secretary to H.R.H. The Prince of Wales

29th April 1997

Dear Mr Hack,

Thank you for your recent letter in which you asked for an interview with The Prince William and a photo opportunity. I am afraid I must decline your request, both The Prince of Wales and Diana, Princess of Wales want to protect Prince William's privacy as far as is possible whilst he is so young. Whilst that is not always possible, a decision has been taken that Prince William will not give interviews.

I am sorry to send you this disappointing reply but I hope you understand why it is important that during the short time that Prince William is being educated he is protected as much as possible from the media spotlight.

Yours sincerely,

Sandy Henney

THE WHITE HOUSE
WASHINGTON

August 5, 1997

Mr. Jefferson Hack
Editor
Dazed & Confused
112-116 Old Street
London, EC1V 9BD
England

Dear Mr. Hack:

Thank you for your recent letter. Chelsea Clinton appreciates the many letters and invitations she receives. However, her activities this summer in preparation for college this fall preclude her participation in any additional undertakings.

Thank you again for writing.

Sincerely yours,

Alice J. Pushkar
Director of Correspondence
for the First Lady

Jefferson Hack

DAZED 34

EDITORIAL
Editor Jefferson Hack
Art Editor Mark Sanders
Associate Editor Damian Lazarus
Assistant Editor Rachel Newsome
Contributing Editor Features Michael Fordham
Contributing Editor Film Wendy Ide
Contributing Editor Alix Sharkey
Assistant Art Editor Roger Tatley
Copy Editor Simon McAusland
Internet Editor Caroline Lambie e-mail caroline@imaginator.com
Editorial Assistants Jamie Oliver, Nicky Wise

PHOTOGRAPHY
Creative Director Rankin
Represented by EGP for photography Tel. 0171 359 1828; for videos by Kudos Tel. 0171 287 0097.
Photographic Director Philip Poynter
Assistant Photo Editor Deirdre O'Callaghan
Senior Photographic Assistant Courtney Hamilton
Photographic Production Jamie
Picture Researcher Paola Cimmino
Photographic Assistants Dennis, Abi Dillon, Iris, Anna Porter, Helen Rhodes

DESIGN
Art Director Molson Deckard Represented by Hughes Behrendt Tel.0181.960.1177 e-mail tekken@confused.co.uk
Design Bret Easton Ellis
Design Assistance Agathe Jacquillat
Troubleshooter Phil Bicker

FASHION
Direct line 0171 490 7117
Fashion Director Katie Grand
Contributing Fashion Editors Katy England, Alister Mackie, Camilla Bidault-Waddington
Fashion Deputies Miranda Robson, Simon Robins, Jo Russell
Fashion Writer Claire Belhassine
Fashion Assistant Laura Rule

ADVERTISING & SPONSORSHIP
Direct line 0171 336 8272
Advertising Sponsorship Director Andrew King
Advertising Manager Kate Monro

PRODUCTION
Production Editor Lotte Ould
Production Manager Stevie Savigear

INTERVIEWS
Tim Barr, Dave Beech, D'Afro, Jil Derryberry, Sarah Edwards, Chris Ewell-Sutton, Cerith Wyn Evans, Rosemary A. Grillo, Kate Hardie, Martin Herbert, Wendy Ide, Susan Irvine, Rita Johnson, Peter Lucas, Anita Liu, Dorian Lynskey, Stuart Hoerdner, Rupert Howe, Helen Mead, Martin McGeown, Paul Moody, Gregor Muir, Rachel Newsome, Anita Pallenberg, Ian Penman, Judith Palmer, Harriet Quick, Peter J. Relic, John Robb, Zoe Richardson, Jon Savage, Ron Rom Scatpelle, Catherine Williams.

PICTURES
Damon Almond, Adrian Arbib, Evan Bernard, Richard Billingham, Grace Cobb, Deirdre O'Callaghan, Ellen Cantor, Dean Chalkley, Jake and Dinos Chapman, Marina Chavez, Liz Collins, Steve Chandler, Andrew Cotterill, Katy England, Angus Fairhurst, Douglas Gordon, Maurice Gutten, Mark Guthrie, Courtney Hamilton, Susan Hiller, Damien Hirst, Martina Hoogland Ivanow, Danny Hole, Barry J. Holmes, Peter Kennard, Barbara Kruger, Marcello Krasilic, Abigail Lane, Tom Luddington, Alister Mackie, Philippe McClelland, Joshua Neville, Lucy Orta, Toby McFarlan Pond, Angus Mill, Fred Offray, Martin Parr, Dennis Pennis, Poros, Raymond Pettibon, Phil Poynter, Marc Quinn, Rankin, Jeff Riedel, Nicola Schwartz, Francesca Sorrenti, Paolo Solari, Sam Taylor-Wood, Charlotte TDP, Errol Thomas, Mike Thomas, Donna Trope, Nick Waplington, Gillian Wearing, Justin Westover, Jane and Louise Wilson, Nick Wilson.

Thanks to Roy and Anne Waddell, Meela brittle @ Positive Management, Jay, Suzie and Paste @ EGP. The Brief, David James @ David James Assoc, Bruno at Cafe Luna, Chantal @ Warp, Len Worrell @ PFC, John Murphy, Rachel Buckley, John, Barb and everyone @ Johno's. Bernie Conway, Frieda Bailey, Tracey Ellis, Eric and Jason @ L?i, Izzy, Katie and Olivia @ Z Photographic, Adrian Carr, Red James, Tibor Kalman, James Lynch, Nathan Constantino, Amanda Patterson, Michael @ Pubfolio, Steve, Simon and Gary @ Direct Lighting, Ollie Waadt, Rex Webb, Abbie, Mark Wilson, Alex Betts @ The Betts Partnership, Kevin and Nigel @ Lloyds Bank, Piccadilly.

Publishers Rankin Waddell & Peter Kravitz
Managing Editors Jefferson Hack, Rankin & Ian C. Taylor
Assistants to the Publisher Sandra Barron, Pam Nolan
Publishing Manager Susanne Waddell
Distribution and Marketing Manager Alex C. Faljone
Marketing Assistant Cristina Nunziata
Office and Gallery Assistant Vanessa Eley
UK Distribution & Overseas Distribution MMC Tel. 01483 211222.
Press Enquiries The Blak Agency Tel. 0181 960 1462 Fax. 0181 964 1355

112. Old Street. London EC1V 9BD Tel. 0171 336 0766 Fax. 0171 336 0966
Web address: www.confused.co.uk / e-mail dazed@confused.co.uk

DAZED

INTRRR ODUCT ION

The contents page of a magazine is of fairly limited use unless the designer's commitment to orientating the reader continues throughout the publication: a number of devices to aid navigation are at the designer's disposal, and they fall into two groups: those whose function is implicit, and those whose function is explicit.

Into the first category fall such techniques as the use of varying paper stocks or colour printing and section-specific typographic styling. The first two are examples of ways in which designers can distinguish sections of the magazine from one another; the third also performs this function, but also guides the reader around the pages themselves, from signalling the start of an article with a bold headline to identifying a change of subject within a continuous block of copy through the use of a bold highlight.

The more explicit aids to navigation are to be found both on the peripheries of the page and in the middle of the articles themselves. The most obvious examples are page numbers; the style adopted for page numbering should be consistent and make clear sense: the page number should appear in the same place on each page and should be easily found. Many magazines omit page numbers from advertising pages, but this sometimes makes it hard for the reader to find what they are looking for. If articles have to be split for reasons of space, the reader should be told on which page the rest of the article can be found, and the remainder of the article should tell readers which page, as well as which article, it follows on from. As well as page numbers, many magazines use section heads – which tell the reader which part of the magazine they are in – or running heads (abbreviated headlines which appear on each page of an article) to remind the reader which specific article, perhaps within a themed section, they are reading.

This page is a door

Other 'tools' frequently used by magazine designers include a set of icons to denote the start of an article, the continuation of an article on the next page, the start and end of an article. For these to be effective they should also be obvious and preferably familiar: it is an established convention, for example, that the magazine's initial in a square block denotes the end of an article.

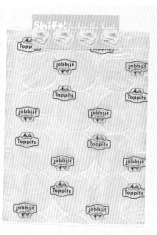

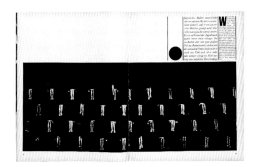

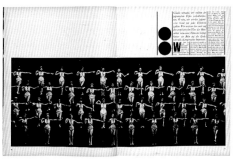

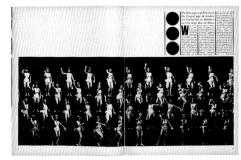

Emigre
Issue: 22, 1992
Art director:
Rudy Vanderlans
USA

Graphics International
Issue: 56, 1998
Design:
Andy Jennings
UK

Emigre
Issue: 19, 1991
Art director:
Rudy Vanderlans
USA

Twen
Issue date: 1962
Art director:
Willy Fleckhaus
Germany

Shift
Art director:
Anja Lutz
Germany

Twen
Issue date: 1962
Art director:
Willy Fleckhaus
Germany

Twen
Issue date: 1962
Art director:
Willy Fleckhaus
Germany

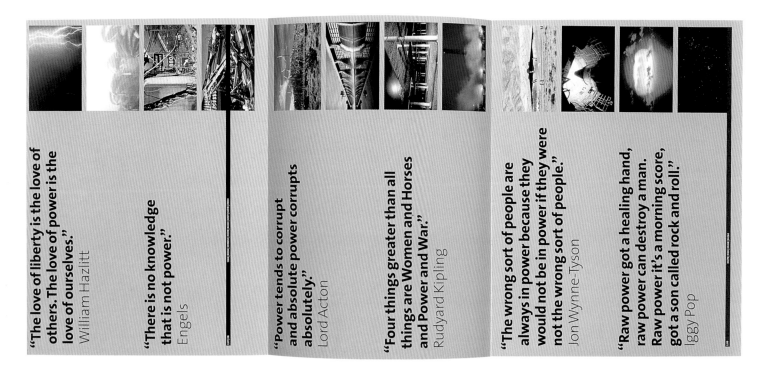

"The love of liberty is the love of others. The love of power is the love of ourselves."
William Hazlitt

"There is no knowledge that is not power."
Engels

"Power tends to corrupt and absolute power corrupts absolutely."
Lord Acton

"Four things greater than all things are Women and Horses and Power and War."
Rudyard Kipling

"The wrong sort of people are always in power because they would not be in power if they were not the wrong sort of people."
Jon Wynne-Tyson

"Raw power got a healing hand, raw power can destroy a man. Raw power it's a morning score, got a son called rock and roll."
Iggy Pop

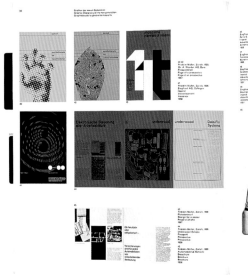

dFusion
Issue: 2, 1998
Art director:
Struktur Design
UK

Neue Graphik
Issue: 2/1959
Art directors:
Richard P. Lohse
J. Müller-Brockmann
Hans Neuberg
Carlo L. Vivarelli
Switzerland

Divider pages are occasionally used in magazines to announce either a change of section or the start of anew, major article. Where space is at a premium, as it is on most magazines, their use signifies the importance of the information highlighted and creates a sense of pace and rhythm throughout the publication. Dividers can either take the form of a double page spread, or more commonly, a left hand page given over to illustration, with the start of the article facing it on the right. In these instances, the 'divider' is arguably no different to the illustration facing the start of an article on the left hand page. Subconsciously, however, the reader notices that the article itself begins after the divider, and recognises the page for what it is – an indulgence. Even where the divider carries a title or standfirst, its positioning suggests that its function is as much to create breathing space for the reader as to illustrate the text that follows it.

The *RSA Journal,* the in-house magazine of the Royal Society of Arts, uses left hand page illustrations to great effect. As a house magazine, the *RSA Journal* carries little advertising, and as most articles are text heavy, the divider pages both punctuate and add colour to the magazine. Similarly, the US-based design magazine *I.D.* prefaces its major features with a specially commissioned illustration which refers to the content of the article. Through the sacrifice of a valuable editorial page, the designer communicates to the reader that the following content is an important part of the magazine.

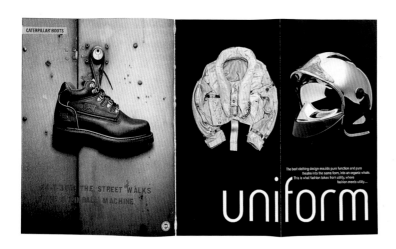

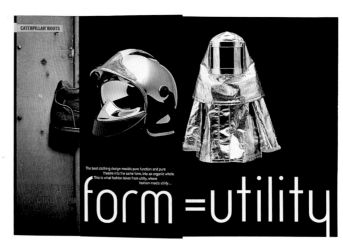

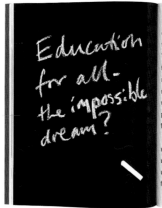

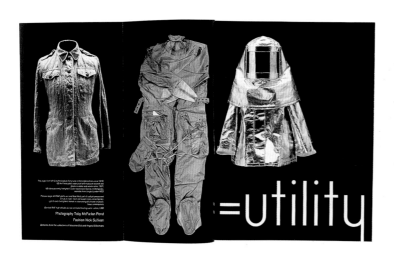

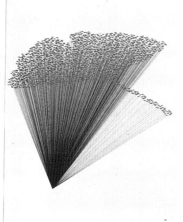

**Arena Homme Plus
Issue:
Autumn/Winter 1996
Art director:
Boris Bencic
UK**

**Arena Homme Plus
Issue:
Autumn/Winter 1996
Art director:
Boris Bencic
UK**

**Arena Homme Plus
Issue:
Autumn/Winter 1996
Art director:
Boris Bencic
UK**

**RSA Journal
Issue: 2 | 4 1998
Art director:
Mike Dempsey
UK**

**I.D.
Issue: Nov 1998
Art director:
Luke Hayman
USA**

**I.D.
Issue: Sep/Oct 1996
Art director:
Anthony Arefin
USA**

Section changes

The prolific editorial designer Roger Black once set ten rules for magazine design. The tenth was 'get lumpy' – distribute content throughout the magazine and even on the page itself in a way that will surprise and excite the reader. Considerations to do with the distribution of content are dealt with more extensively in the advertising and pagination section of this book. But given that content will be spread throughout the magazine, and may well vary in type and tone in the process, it is left to the designer to add some sense of logic to its presentation.

At a basic level, most magazines will be split into features and supplementaries – the features being the longer articles stretching over several pages or spreads

and the supplementaries being the shorter items – news or listings, for example – at the front and back of the magazine. It is standard practice to distinguish between the two using design, and while there are no fixed rules for doing so, examination of a random sample of publications suggests that the use of wider columns for text, different typefaces, longer standfirsts and bigger headlines for features are the norm.

Some magazines go even further: *Arena*, for example, uses a completely different paper stock for its 'something else' section, as well as different typefaces, headline fonts and illustration styles, while magazines such as *World Architecture* use background tints to identify certain sections.

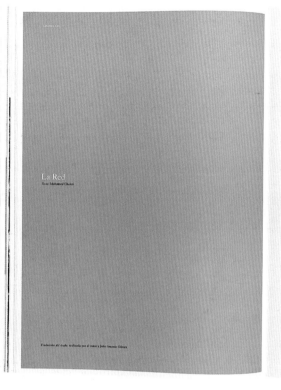

Matador
Issue: 'B', 1996
Art director:
Fernando Gutiérrez
Spain

World Architecture
Issue: Apr 1997
Art director:
Struktur Design
UK

The supreme achievement of symbiosis
Kisho Kurokawa architect & associates

World Architecture profiles the work of Kisho
Kurokawa, an architect whose achievements over a
35-year career mark him out as one of the twentieth
century's architectural greats. The first overseas
architect to be selected as Honourary Fellow at both the
Royal Institute of British Architects, in London and the
Ordre des Architectes in Paris, Kurokawa's reputation for
both his built work and for the diversity of issues and
theories addressed within it is unsurpassed. Peter
Wislocki went to meet the man for whom building is a
vehicle for philosophical expression.

Interior view of the cone
at the Ehime Prefectural
Museum of General
Science, Shikoku Island,
Japan. The cone, a
primary form used
regularly by Kurokawa,
communicates notions
of centrality and
cohesion

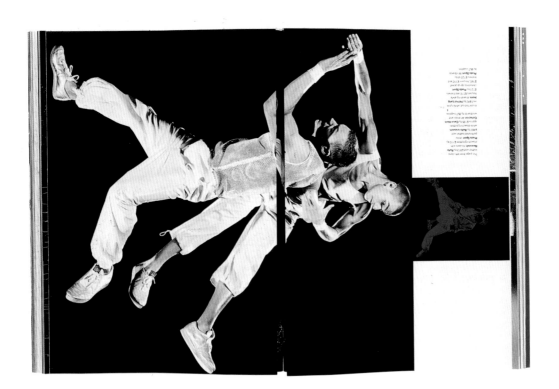

**Arena Homme Plus
Issue:
Spring/Summer 1999
Art director:
Steven Baillie
Design and
photography:
Fabien Baron
UK**

**Arena Homme Plus
Issue:
Spring/Summer 1999
Art director:
Steven Baillie
Design and
photography:
Fabien Baron
UK**

**Neue Graphik
Issue: 1/1958
Art directors:
Richard P. Lohse
J. Müller-Brockmann
Hans Neuberg
Carlo L. Vivarelli
Switzerland**

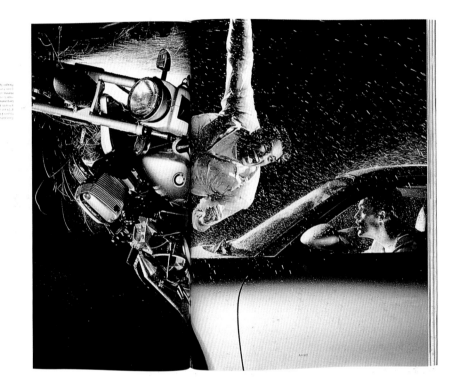

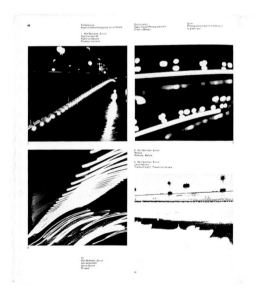

Rovigon | ROCHE | Tonicum in mittleren und höheren Jahren

The terms to describe the opening lines of an article are imprecise. Many journalists and designers refer to the few lines that summarise the content of an article as the headline. More accurately, however, the headline is the title of the article, and the few lines following it are a 'standfirst'.

The standfirst takes many different forms. Sometimes it is the first paragraph of the body copy of the article itself, perhaps picked out in bold. In other cases, it can be as minimal as a credit for writer and photographer. Usually, however, the standfirst is a few lines long, and stands alone, acting as a bridge between the headline and the actual text of the article.

It performs two essential functions: first, as a precis of what is to follow (who the interview is with, what the journalist is intending to argue) it gives the reader an idea of whether or not they should continue to read the article. If the standfirst sounds promising, they will give the article a go; if not, they'll turn the page. Second, it orientates the reader, forming part of a hierarchy of information – headline, standfirst, copy – that makes the reading experience easier. As is discussed elsewhere in this book, even for the most literate people, reading is an essentially stressful activity, requiring an unnatural level of concentration and co-ordination. Consequently, any small measures writers and designers can take to entice readers to persevere will pay dividends. It is for that reason that art directors use larger point sizes, italics, bold faces, colours or other distinguishing features in the standfirst.

Although the job of writing standfirsts falls either to the journalist, the editor, or if there is one, the sub-editor, the art director will usually want to have a hand in decisions on how long it will be, for example. Standfirsts much longer than 40 words, or three or four lines, are self-defeating: they become as off-putting as the body of text they purport to welcome the reader into.

By Jamie Doran and Piers Bizony

Just 108 minutes on April 12, 1961, would turn Yuri Gagarin into the most famous man in the world. Not only was he the first man ever to journey into space, he was also charming, sincere, handsome and more than a match for most of the world leaders and celebrities he would subsequently meet. Too popular, it turned out, for the cold hearts of the emerging Brezhnev regime, who felt threatened by his charisma and determined to plot his downfall

The man who fell to earth

With Timothy Egan

Polygamy. Uncles wedding nieces. Violence. Abuse. Such stories have long been kept behind the closed doors of powerful Mormon clans. Now a group of women have banded together to see these secretive practices aired in court

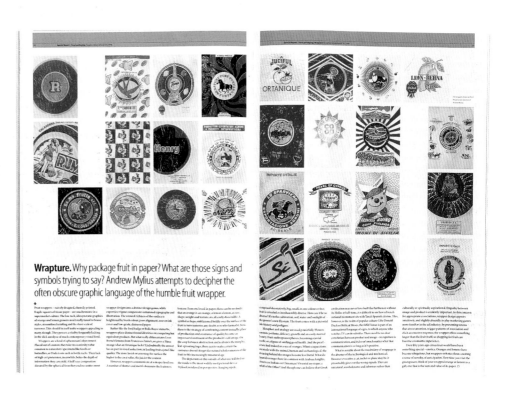

Wrapture. Why package fruit in paper? What are those signs and symbols trying to say? Andrew Mylius attempts to decipher the often obscure graphic language of the humble fruit wrapper.

How an art director decides to identify the authors of an article will depend on a number of factors: Does the identity of the author have a bearing on the validity of the views expressed – an article by Henry Kissinger on US foreign policy, for example. Similarly, does the fact that the writer or photographer has contributed to the publication represent a coup – is the writer a big name in the field, for instance. In those circumstances, an art director may even decide to abandon the magazine's regular credit style for something more prominent or eye-catching.

In the main, however, a system of displaying credit information must be worked out in advance and applied to all parts and issues of the magazine. It must take account of factors such as whether all pieces of text or images will be identified, or will some go unsigned; the need for flexibility – will some articles be written or illustrated by more than one contributor; the need for supplementary information – will the credit need to carry some biographical detail on the author to explain their perspective or declare their interest?

The number of potential systems is almost infinite: some designers include the writer's name in the standfirst, some bury it at the edge of the page, others still identify the author of an article with just their initials at the end of the copy. In some instances photographers or illustrators are identified by captions next to their pictures, instead of sharing space with the writer at the head of the article. This is a subject on which the editor, and probably the contributors themselves, will certainly have a view: beyond the danger to fragile egos, poorly handled credit information can fail to alert the reader to a magazine's most valuable asset: the reputation and quality of its contributors.

"I was in Scotland doing a post-grad at Edinburgh University. My hobby was kinetic art. I needed a 'sound' to complete a work. After messing around with unsuccessful electronic attempts, I was reminded of a sound I had known since childhood; telegraph poles. By chance, one night in Mull, camping, I found myself listening to the music of a telegraph pole which stood next to where I had parked the campervan in the middle of the night...pure serendipity. It took me the next six years to develop the means of recording and composing from this sound, mostly in a remote part of Western Australia where I had bought for ten dollars a kilometre of abandoned telegraph wires."

Such a chance discovery brought Alan a new form of sound for his kinetic art experiments, but the realisation of the capacity for telegraph wires to literally sing in something akin to music was not far behind. "This was not just sound, but music, and a music attaining perfection but not of human design. At first I thought if I recorded long enough I might capture a perfect symphony, played by wind and chance alone, but that was not to be. I had to become a 'composer' to realise the full potential of 'wire music' as it has become known.

"Because it is not the wire responsible for such extraordinary effects, I presume it must be the properties of the wind itself. Indeed I have observed many times that apparently identical wind velocities and directions can result in effects varying from total silence to cacophony, pure harmony to unison. Obviously tension matters, but only when it is changing contrary to the usual wisdom about string tension and frequency. Thus temperature fluctuations matter, as when the sun goes behind a cloud or a cold wind blows.

"I believe, but without evidence, that the air flow of a wind may possess a variety of structures such as laminar verses

material and was immediately transfixed. Indeed the first time any listener encounters 'wire music' they are struck by the elegant alien beauty and dizzying depths of the recordings. They are truly unlike anything you will have ever heard. Darrin soon released the first album of Alan's work as Dorobo 008, Primal Image. The release garnered much positive attention internationally with left field artists like Godflesh, Techno Animal, Witchman, Paul Schütze and Kevin Martin heaping praise upon it.

The idea of a remix, or as it later became known a demix, project was mentioned to several of Darrin's associates|friends| collaborators and several months later the finished product has arrived. Entitled Night Passage, it is a compilation of four disparate reconstructions of Alan's raw music by Japanese ambient technoist Ryoji Ikeda, isolationist Thomas Köner, Brian Williams and Paul Haslinger of arcane soundscape pioneers Lustmord, and the German experimental electronic composer Bernhard Günter. Each was given a small sample of the material and a free hand. The results are astonishing. All of the remixers had extremely positive views on Primal Image and were keen to look into the possibilities inherent in 'wire music'.

"At first I thought that there was no need to remix – it's enough to be as it is. It's wonderful," explained Ryoji Ikeda, "so the most important thing is my respect for Alan's original materials while remixing." Brian Williams had similar feelings. "Our initial response was that of amusement – not because we considered the album (Primal Image) a joke, but it amused us greatly that both its ambience and content were far superior to a whole series of releases by self important 'experimental| noise|industrial' bands!"

"I remember being really curious to know what the original

within the source material, with all the limitations inherent in using a very specific sound, it made it a worthwhile challenge," says Brian. "From the beginning we felt that the original recordings, if anything, had a sense of emptiness, and that with any reconstruction and processing we carried out we should enhance the feeling of melancholy. We did consider the fact that the other contributors would most likely concentrate on the drone aspect of the recordings, and to make it both more interesting for ourselves and more varied as an album, we decided to introduce a hint of melody along with heavily treated dialogue."

"Actually, I think limitation is and always was a most important part in making music. In this case, the wire recordings could be seen as black and white photography verses colour; it's just a more narrow spectrum, giving it at the same time more atmospheric value and style," agrees Paul.

What are Alan's views on the altered versions available on Night Passage?

"The experiment is a success. I do not mean necessarily that the sound|music is good, that is not for me to say as I know next to nothing about music. But from a point of view of the creation of a self-evolving musical organism about which I am a highly enthusiastic proponent, this experiment has much to teach. Firstly, the dedication of the five composers to such an experiment. It is not an easy challenge to be given such alien material as some recordings of a medium which I know takes so long to master, and to be told to make something worthy of a CD. Each composer in his own way created something magnificent. I was astounded by how different from my own expectations the four works were. The focus and emphasis of each showed me how little I have heard in my own ear of all

---

Alan Lamb is an Australian scientist. He is also the creator of the phenomena known as 'wire music'. By milking telegraph wires in the Outback and recording the results, he has invented a new form of sound. Australian label Dorobo, who released his initial recordings, have now put together an album of 'de'mixes, entitled Night Passage, this brings together leading edge leftfielders Thomas Köner, Brian Lustmord, Ryoji Ikeda and Bernhard Günter. These unique interpretations push wire music to new dimensions.

---

turbulent and more subtle things. Astronomers describe a good viewing night as crystalline as if referring to some structure of the atmosphere unrelated to the character of the wind. By way of concord, I have observed that at night, when the wires are singing at their most pure, the stars are at their brightest and yet there may seem to be little or no wind. It is mysterious."

At the time of his discovery, Alan was working as a neuroscientist although he dismisses any links between his scientific background and his leanings toward both kinetic art and experimental sound. He does allow that his training did help him in devising recording methodology, but it was the musician in him which provided the all important link. "I am not a trained musician though I do have a good ear. I do wonder how much greater it all might have been, indeed might yet be, if I were to be collaborating with a trained musician. Primal Image is already perfection to my ear. But who knows what is still to come."

Darrin Verhagen, label owner of Melbourne's Dorobo and recording entity under the Shinjuku Thief banner, heard the raw

sources were and how much of what I heard was an actual composition. I was impressed by the kind of space that was opened up by these sounds coming out of my speakers," comments Benhard Günter. "The idea of a remix was to use the source materials and compose a piece of my own but when I first tried using them, this proved 100 times more difficult than I had originally thought. The material is so dense and rich that it seemed almost impossible to use it in any way other than a documentary approach. My ideas changed from a simple composition using the sources to a complete deconstruction| reconstruction strategy – it is so hard to recognise any of the sources in the finished piece. I actually like the way it has turned out, even if it bears little resemblence to what it's supposed to be a remix of!"

Brian and Paul of Lustmord also found the whole experience a unique challenge.

"Being asked to remix a series of recordings of telegraph wires is an interesting proposition, the kind that it's difficult to say no to. Given that we were restricted to the sounds available

that wire music can give, and that only in the small sample of material which I gave to the composers. What if they had access to all the hundreds of hours of recordings? Or a wind organ to play themselves, together or alone?"

Night Passage has been released through Dorobo, distributed by Impetus in the UK. A further album of Alan's raw wire material will be released shortly as Dorobo 013. Bernhard Günter has a new collaborative album with John Duncan titled Home out on his own label, Trente Oiseaux and is involved in another remix project reconstructing Merzbow for Blast First. Ryoji Ikeda has completed a second album for Touch and a third for Staalplaat. He is currently recording with the Japanese art group Dumb Type. Lustmord are at work on their next album and the second Arecibo release, while Paul Halsinger has a new recording out through Side Effects under the name of Coma Virus. Thomas Köner's Porter Ricks atmospheric|rhythmic project with Andy Mellwig has just released two 12" singles on Force Inc. and a 10" on Barooni.

Leigh Neville

We have 10 copies of the Night Passage CD to give away to the first 10 people requesting it on a postcard. Let us know what you think.

The Guardian Weekend
Issue: Mar 1998
Art director:
Mark Porter
UK

Observer Life
Issue: Apr 1999
Art director:
Wayne Ford
UK

Graphics International
Issue: May 1996
Art director:
MetaDesign
UK

Immerse
Issue: 002, 1997
Art director:
Struktur Design
UK

**Interview
with Mark Porter
Pagination and advertising
Typography
Captions**

Structure

**Interview
with Mark Porter**

When Mark Porter won a prestigious D&AD Award for *The Guardian* newspaper's *Weekend* supplement, it confirmed his position as one of the pre-eminent editorial designers in the UK. That he has made it to the top in such a fiercely competitive area of design is made all the more remarkable by the fact that Porter has no formal design training: he left Oxford University with a first class degree in modern languages, and for want of anything better to do, took a job selling advertising space on *Decanter*, a magazine for the wine trade. In his own words, he 'was terrible at selling ads,' and quickly became aware that a career in the business side of advertising was not for him. But before leaving the magazine, he took the liberty of redesigning it in his spare time. 'At that time I knew absolutely nothing about design,' he recollects now, 'but luckily they knew nothing too, so they said "Yes" to the redesign.' Porter stayed at *Decanter* for another year as art director, before moving to Redwood Publishing to work under its art director Mike Lackersteen, the first in a line of 'mentor' figures who throughout Porter's career have provided him with the best sort of on-the-job training.

**Cover of
The Guardian
Weekend
Jan 1999**

**Cover of
The Guardian
Weekend
May 1997**

**Spread from
Direction**

**Spread from
ES Magazine
Oct 1992**

Redwood Publishing's selling point is that it produces contract or customer magazines with the same editorial, design and production values as a commercial publisher. Porter started work on *Expression!*, the American Express magazine, for which art director Mike Lackersteen had won a D&AD Award the year before. Working with Lackersteen involved a sharp learning curve, an experience that has been repeated throughout Porter's subsequent career: 'It was quite tough. He's a very nice guy, very charming guy, but he wants everything to be absolutely brilliant. A lot of the people I've worked for have been very, very demanding people, and a lot of the time, when you're working for people like that, you're not actually that happy; sometimes you just want to forget about it and go home. But if it's not right, you just have to do it again and again until you get it right. Working for people like that I've learned that it's really important to keep going, dragging the last nuances out of something. Time and time again, you've got to the stage where you think a layout or a magazine is 95 per cent there, and it then takes them to say, "Look, I think it's really important that you push it until it's absolutely perfect".'

Having survived the rigours of Redwood and customer magazine publishing, Porter's next move was to the business publisher Haymarket Publishing. Again, the presence of a well-respected senior figure was instrumental in Porter's decision to take the job: 'Haymarket was a trade publisher with a great design tradition, but the main reason I went there was at that time they had Clive Irving as editorial director. He'd been involved with the launch of [the advertising trade weekly] *Campaign* in the '60s, worked at *The Sunday Times* with Harry Evans, and helped set up *The Sunday Times Magazine*. He was not an art director, he was very much a journalist, but he was incredibly inspiring, and it was him who convinced me that you could do business magazines and still make them exciting. He was another of those mentor figures.'

Porter remained at Haymarket for three years, starting first on *Marketing* magazine, before moving on to *Campaign*. Simultaneously he began to design *Direction*, the now-defunct monthly glossy for the design and advertising industries. Porter used it as a test ground for new ideas, and in that way it too contributed to his development of a unique, personal approach. This was aided, in part, by his pairing with a sympathetic and encouraging editor, Jane Lamacraft: 'You can be the most brilliant art director in the world, but if you don't have a good relationship with your editor, then there's a limit to what you can achieve. That's one of the reasons that I think we've managed to do some good things with *Weekend*. Most editors wouldn't have let me use that picture of the Spice Girls on the cover, and would have insisted that you had to see their faces. But that's an example of an occasion where it takes an editor with a bit of vision to enable you to do your thing.'

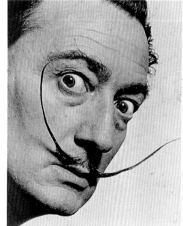

When a man with a Zapata moustache gave a lecture in a diving suit, it could mean only one thing: Salvador Dali was in town. MEREDITH ETHERINGTON-SMITH recounts the surrealist's London life and loves

Hello, Dali

mondino

on the spot When MTV banned Jean Baptiste Mondino's steamy Justify My Love video, Madonna's favourite pro-video director went un-directory, shunned all interviews and retreated into an uncharacteristic silence. Three months on, Direction finally persuaded the multi-talented Monsieur Mondino to break it. Sophie Harscombe met him in his Paris studio, where he revealed all about Paul Anka and Prince, fatherhood and the priesthood, and why he sometimes finds artistes and actors a pain in the arse

Porter's next move was to a magazine where several of today's leading art directors, including Fernando Gutiérrez, Scott Stowell and Gary Koepke have refined their styles – *Colors*. The international magazine funded by the Benetton clothing company was at that time based in Rome and was edited by Tibor Kalman, who had himself art directed *Interview* and *Art Forum* magazines in New York. Working under Kalman proved to be another inspirational, if exhausting, experience: 'It was difficult, but incredibly rewarding,' recalls Porter. 'It was an amazing opportunity that I'll probably never have again. *Colors* was a magazine with as many pages as you wanted, with only two or three ads, and no real limit on how much you spent. You could use any photographer you wanted, although [*Colors*' founder and editorial director] Oliviero Toscani obviously took a lot of the pictures. And there were no rules about what should be in there and how it should be presented.' Porter identifies a few key skills that he learned from working with Kalman on *Colors*: 'One of the things that I had a sense of before, but really learned when I was working with Tibor, is that most people don't really care about graphic design.'

'A lot of the tricks that designers use, or games that you play when you're doing a layout, really don't add anything to the readability of something, or to what most readers see in it. So one of the things that would frustrate me at the start, but eventually I found very rewarding, was that I would be working on something and he'd say "This thing you've done here, it's just a kind of art director's orgasm; nobody's going to notice – take it out and leave what was there". Trying to not think like a graphic designer was a really good thing to learn.' Many of the lessons learned on *Colors* are now evident in Porter's approach to *Weekend*, particularly his concern for readability: 'We'd take a layout apart until just the bare bones were left, and then put a little bit back in, a little joke of the sort that readers really do enjoy – getting a sense of fun into the product without detracting from the seriousness of it. And a lot of Tibor's standard little games were turning something upside down, or playing with scale. It's amazing to watch people look though a magazine that has things like that in it. You just see a little smirk or a little giggle. It doesn't last very long but it adds something to the experience and it's something that makes people bond with the magazine. It's wonderful to see people reading the magazine and enjoying the little bits of entertainment they're being given.'

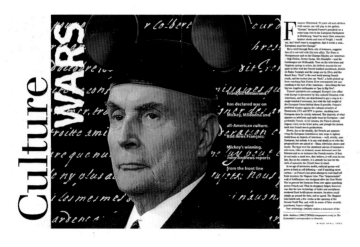

**Spread from
Wired magazine
Apr 1995**

**Spread from
Colors magazine**

**Spread from
Direction magazine**

At *Weekend*, Porter works with a picture editor, Vivian Handley, and relishes the input of someone with a different approach and understanding of photography. But it was at *Colors* under Kalman that he learned an important lesson in the commissioning, selection and use of photography: 'Something I learned from Tibor was to really, really look at pictures. A lot of the time pictures come across your desk, and you look for a few seconds at a few things – composition, contrast, movement – and you are able, almost without engaging your brain, to say "good picture" or "bad picture". If you're doing something with a really big set of pictures, or a really important set of pictures, or a set of pictures where the story is particularly complicated or sensitive, you have to get beyond that and the only way you can do that is by staring at pictures for hours and hours and hours. Tibor used to do this, and encourage me to do it, and now that I've done it, I encourage everybody else to do it, because it is incredible. If you look at a set of pictures you think one thing about it, and then if you keep looking at them for half an hour you think another thing, and if you look for another half an hour they start talking to you, and you get a whole new set of ideas about what they are and how they work. So that was a really valuable skill to learn. At *Colors* a lot of the things we did were quite important;

that's partly what I like about *Weekend*, that we do some serious stories – we've done several stories on miscarriages of justice that have actually helped people get out of jail. The idea that you can do something on a magazine that affects real life is incredible to me, and when you're doing a story like that, you have a responsibility to do it properly, and it goes slightly beyond just being a designer, making things look good. You have to go beyond your set way of doing things and really look deeper.'

Porter is himself now in the role of mentor, as he has two designers working under him at *Weekend*, and is passing along the insights that he has been given along the way. Having risen to the top of his profession, Mark Porter is still as enthusiastic about the business of editorial design as he was when he took it upon himself to redesign a magazine in his spare time, and he is still learning on the job. As he says himself, 'I hope there will be magazines and newspapers left to do for as long as I'm working because it still fascinates me. You can never get bored with it because there are an infinite number of stories that you could be doing. As long as there are words and pictures and ideas, the scope of magazine design is infinite.'

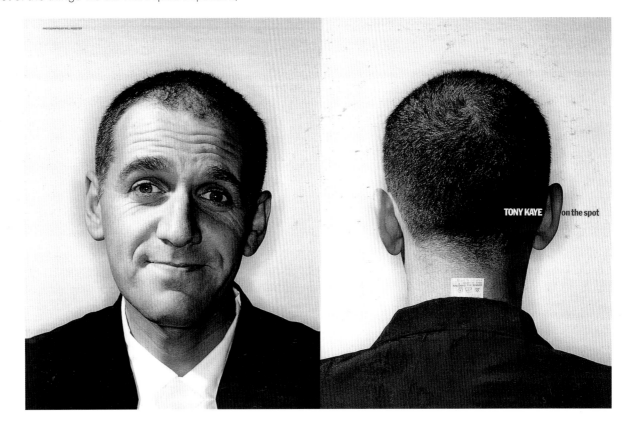

TONY KAYE on the spot

Pagination

According to Oliviero Toscani, the editorial director of *Colors*, 'Making a magazine is like making a concert. To me it's like making a show. So you have to come up with the highs and lows. You have to interest people not just with what you say but also with the way that you say it. You push and pull, you add and detract. It should be a surprise, exactly like reading a book – a real book. But magazines are not usually like that.' The pagination of a magazine – the order in which articles appear, whether they are on half pages, singles or doubles, and the distance between them, usually filled by advertising, gives pace and emphasis to the magazine. Even if it goes without saying that bunching articles at the beginning of the magazine, for example, gives an unbalanced feel to the whole, it may be less obvious that ending one feature on a left hand page and beginning another on the right may feel a little incongruous. While it is standard practice to put the contents page at the start of the magazine, only an understanding of how readers interact with the publication will suggest that there are psychological advantages in saving a good piece of editorial until the end: finish with a bang, not a whimper, the structure of a magazine is essentially linear – it is assumed that the reader will start at the front cover and read through to the back without deviation. Of course, it is recognised that readers do no such thing, and the inclusion of a contents list and page numbers mean that they can easily skip to the bit which they are most interested in if they wish to. But when a magazine is planned, it is generally done on the assumption that readers will begin at the beginning and end, regretfully, at the end.

Pagination must also take account of the wishes of advertisers and the demands of the print process: the total number of pages must be a multiple of four, and if, for example, different paper stocks are used to identify sections, those pages too must be a multiple of four.

Pagination or page planning is an important landmark in the production process of any magazine, though where it comes in the process will vary from title to title. It is a collaborative effort and will usually involve the editor, the art director, the production editor and a representative of the advertising sales department. Each has an interest in obtaining for their work, or their clients, the choicest positions in the magazine. The outcome is dependent on necessary compromise and the determination of the individual.

Advertising
Deciding how the content is arranged throughout the magazine is a team effort: the art director will have an opinion, as will the editor. As will a third party which hitherto has been strangely silent: advertisers. The sale of advertising space is the basis on which most magazines survive financially – cover prices rarely even cover the cost of printing. There are a few exceptions: customer or contract publications, such as Colors, are essentially subsidised by the company which owns them; magazines, which reject all advertising either lose money or have an unusually high cover price. The rest depend on advertising revenue, and consequently those who buy advertising have a lot of clout in certain areas. They may seek to influence the editorial content of the magazine. Failing that (and they don't always fail to do that by any means), they will seek to ensure that their advertising is not placed next to any editorial feature they consider to be damaging to the reputation of their product. Coca-Cola famously produced a list of such positions which included, for example, health stories, good or bad.

Advertisers will also pay more to be in certain parts of the magazine – the inside of covers, the back cover, on a page facing editorial matter or in the first third of the magazine are the types of desirable positions specified. Designers have to be acutely aware of this when considering concepts for a magazine – due to the popularity of the first third of the magazine, as well as advertisements facing editorial matter, it is unlikely that there will be many double page spreads of editorial in the first third of the magazine, for example. It would not be wise, therefore, to attach too much importance to such spreads in dummy plans for the magazine. Some designers have successfully fought for consecutive double page spreads and the like, despite the loss of potential advertising revenue. An unbroken photo-story is a central feature of UK-based style magazine Sleazenation. Similarly, Geoff Waring, art director of Red magazine, convinced the publisher that it was in the interests of the magazine as a whole to have unbroken chunks of editorial up to eight-pages long; it created the impression of luxury and style that would ultimately, it was hoped, attract advertisers in its own right.

Colors
Issue: 1
Editorial director:
Oliviero Toscani
Editor-in-chief:
Tibor Kalman
Art director:
Emily Oberman
USA

Colors
Issue: 26
Editorial director:
Oliviero Toscani
Creative editor:
Adam Broomberg
Designer:
Thomas Hilland
Italy

Arena
Issue: Apr 1999
Art director:
Martin Farran-Lee
UK

Vogue
Issue: Feb 1999
Art director:
Luca Stoppini
Italy

On some magazines, especially trade titles or those that run classified ads, much of the advertising will be designed in-house by the publishing company. On most, however, a pre-prepared design will be supplied by an agency, and the magazine's designers will therefore have no control over what it looks like, even if it clashes violently with the style of the magazine. Most art directors would shrug philosophically and consider this an unavoidable part of publishing life. Not so *Wallpaper*. The UK-based style and interiors magazine returns ads it does not like, asking for rewrites or redesigns before they are allowed between the hallowed covers of the magazine. Ironically, by taking such cares, the *Wallpaper* team safeguards the values that go to make the magazine a prestige product and keep those same advertisers coming back again and again.

In publishing terms, the advertiser is the magazine's client, and the art director is often asked to bear this fact in mind; as mentioned above, advertisers are notoriously sensitive about the environments with which they want to be associated, and several magazines have run into trouble because advertisers were doubtful about the look of the magazine.

Although both *Beach Culture*, designed by David Carson, and the first incarnation of *Arena*, designed by Neville Brody, are now recognised as landmarks in the development of editorial design, and found widespread approval among readers, advertisers were suspicious of the unusual designs, threatening the financial security of both magazines. Writing about the impact of *Arena*'s design, the critic David Cook noted that it is often assumed that advertisers were queuing up to associate themselves with this outlandish new magazine. This was not the case:

'The advertising revenue was not simply there for the taking, and the content and design of the magazine did not just pander to the moods set by the marketeers...'[1] Nevertheless, its publishers had faith in their product, and *Arena* still exists to this day. Its content and design, while unfamiliar, were adopted by its audience, and like Brody's earlier work at *The Face*, went on to influence the look of advertising even outside the cloistered world of magazine publishing. Likewise, David Carson's editorial design has been hugely influential in all areas of visual communications, from commercials to record sleeves. The belated acceptance of his work by the advertising industry, however, came too late to save *Beach Culture*.

[1]Redesigning Men:
Arena Magazine, Image and Identity, published in 'Communicating Design: Essays in Visual Communication', ed., Teal Triggs; Batsford, 1995

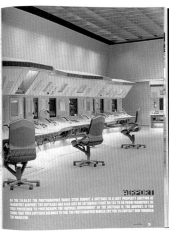

Sleazenation
Issue: Nov 1998
Art director:
Nick Booth
UK

Madison
Issue: Jan 1999
Art director:
Jacqueline J. Galler
USA

Advertorials

Advertorials or advertising features or 'promotions' are advertisements dressed up as editorial. Advertisers pay a premium to have their ads made to look as though it were part of the editorial content, thereby giving readers the impression that the product has been endorsed by the magazine. In such instances the copy may even be written by the magazine's own staff, and the page will almost certainly be laid out by the magazine's own designers. While advertorials should always be identified as such, some designers devise other, subtle ways to set them apart from the rest of the magazine, without denying the advertiser what they have paid for. Page tints, borders, the prominent positioning of a company logo and the use of different typefaces are four such methods.

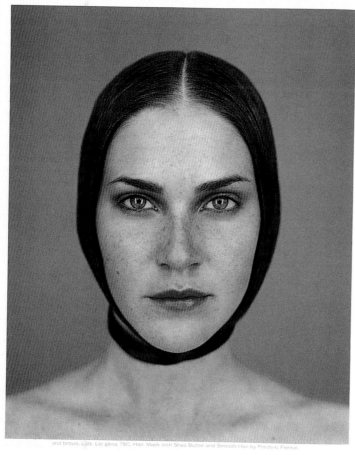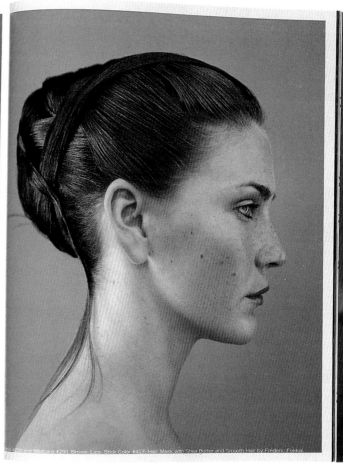

and brows. Lips: Lip gloss 78C. Hair: Mask with Shea Butter and Smooth Hair by Frédéric Fekkai.

and Manicure #29. Brows. Lips: Stick Color #417. Hair: Mask with Shea Butter and Smooth Hair by Frédéric Fekkai.

The 26th issue of *Colors* magazine carried an interesting and illuminating article on the nature of reading and the role played by carefully considered typography in encouraging readers to tackle an article. Most readers, however, would have finished the issue none the wiser on these matters, having elected to skip the article. That was the point. Laid out in a single typeface, and a single weight, in black type on a white background, in a single column the width of the page, with no accompanying images, the article looked impregnable and difficult to read. It was, and those who did struggle through to the end could easily believe the claim made by the writer that given the average human being's eight second attention span, they were virtually alone in having done so.

The *Colors* article was an extreme example, as no concessions had been made to create a pleasant reading experience. But in general, it is worth remembering that readers of magazines will ignore pages styled in a way that the same reader would find perfectly acceptable in a book. Unrelieved columns of text, lines containing more than 60 or 70 characters and an overall typographic sameness of appearance – from headline to captions – are all extremely off-putting in a magazine context. Nevertheless, most magazines feature articles up to 5,000 words long: they are the backbone of the magazine, its principal selling point and the content against which most advertising is sold. It is therefore of critical importance that the designer should make them palatable through judicious use of type and image.

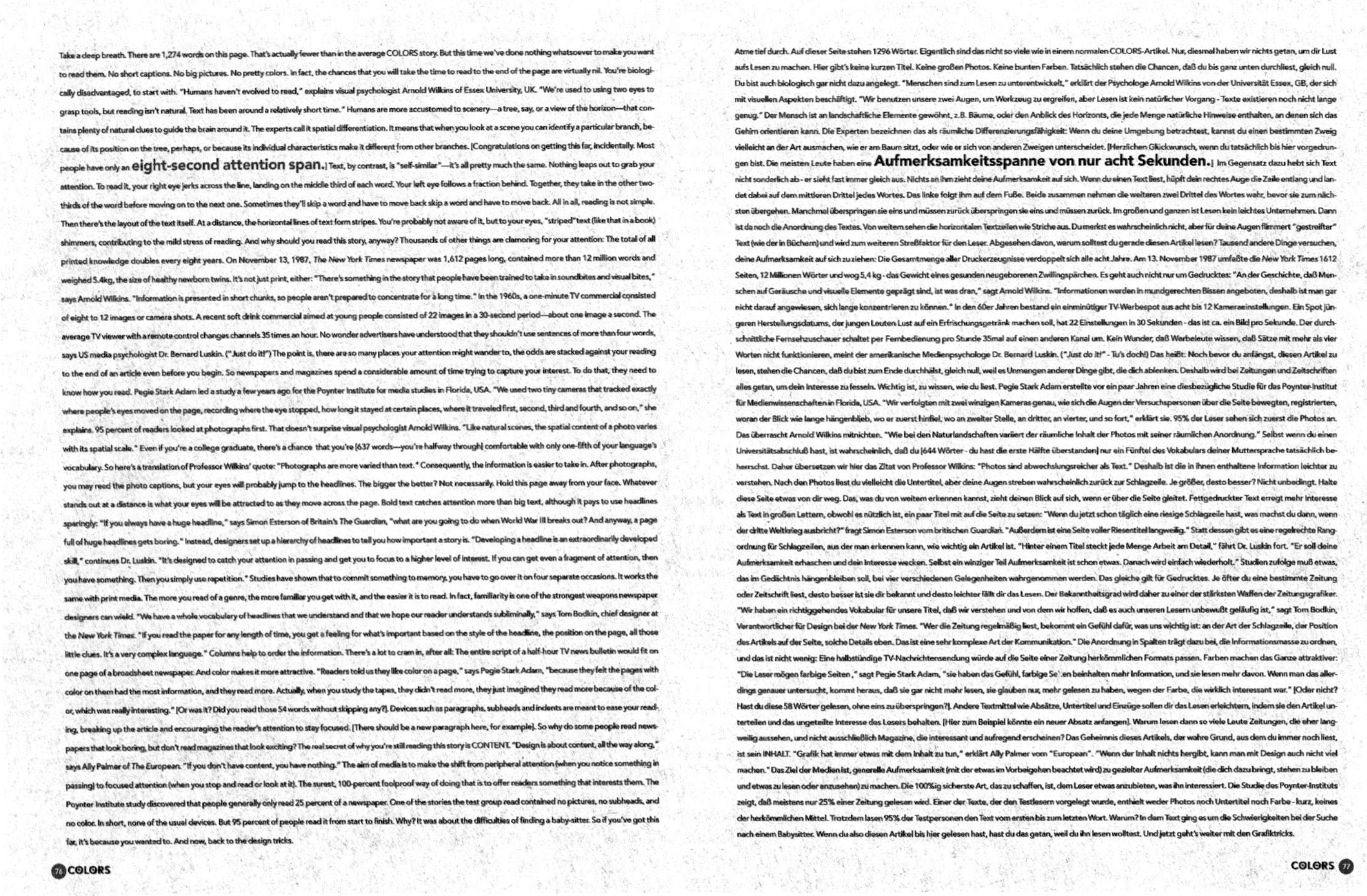

Take a deep breath. There are 1,274 words on this page. That's actually fewer than in the average COLORS story. But this time we've done nothing whatsoever to make you want to read them. No short captions. No big pictures. No pretty colors. In fact, the chances that you will take the time to read to the end of the page are virtually nil. You're biologically disadvantaged, to start with. "Humans haven't evolved to read," explains visual psychologist Arnold Wilkins of Essex University, UK. "We're used to using two eyes to grasp tools, but reading isn't natural. Text has been around a relatively short time." Humans are more accustomed to scenery—a tree, say, or a view of the horizon—that contains plenty of natural clues to guide the brain around it. The experts call it spatial differentiation. It means that when you look at a scene you can identify a particular branch, because of its position on the tree, perhaps, or because its individual characteristics make it different from other branches. [Congratulations on getting this far, incidentally. Most people have only an **eight-second attention span.**] Text, by contrast, is "self-similar"—it's all pretty much the same. Nothing leaps out to grab your attention. To read it, your right eye jerks across the line, landing on the middle third of each word. Your left eye follows a fraction behind. Together, they take in the other two-thirds of the word before moving on to the next one. Sometimes they'll skip a word and have to move back skip a word and have to move back. All in all, reading is not simple. Then there's the layout of the text itself. At a distance, the horizontal lines of text form stripes. You're probably not aware of it, but to your eyes, "striped" text (like that in a book) shimmers, contributing to the mild stress of reading. And why should you read this story, anyway? Thousands of other things are clamoring for your attention: The total of all printed knowledge doubles every eight years. On November 13, 1987, *The New York Times* newspaper was 1,612 pages long, contained more than 12 million words and weighed 5.4kg, the size of healthy newborn twins. It's not just print, either: "There's something in the story that people have been trained to take in soundbites and visual bites," says Arnold Wilkins. "Information is presented in short chunks, so people aren't prepared to concentrate for a long time." In the 1960s, a one-minute TV commercial consisted of eight to 12 images or camera shots. A recent soft drink commercial aimed at young people consisted of 22 images in a 30-second period—about one image a second. The average TV viewer with a remote control changes channels 35 times an hour. No wonder advertisers have understood that they shouldn't use sentences of more than four words, says US media psychologist Dr. Bernard Luskin. ("Just do it!") The point is, there are so many places your attention might wander to, the odds are stacked against your reading to the end of an article even before you begin. So newspapers and magazines spend a considerable amount of time trying to capture your interest. To do that, they need to know how you read. Pegie Stark Adam led a study a few years ago for the Poynter Institute for media studies in Florida, USA. "We used two tiny cameras that tracked exactly where people's eyes moved on the page, recording where the eye stopped, how long it stayed at certain places, where it traveled first, second, third and fourth, and so on," she explains. 95 percent of readers looked at photographs first. That doesn't surprise visual psychologist Arnold Wilkins. "Like natural scenes, the spatial content of a photo varies with its spatial scale." Even if you're a college graduate, there's a chance that you're [637 words—you're halfway through] comfortable with only one-fifth of your language's vocabulary. So here's a translation of Professor Wilkins' quote: "Photographs are more varied than text." Consequently, the information is easier to take in. After photographs, you may read the photo captions, but your eyes will probably jump to the headlines. The bigger the better? Not necessarily. Hold this page away from your face. Whatever stands out at a distance is what your eyes will be attracted to as they move across the page. Bold text catches attention more than big text, although it pays to use headlines sparingly: "If you always have a huge headline," says Simon Esterson of Britain's The Guardian, "what are you going to do when World War III breaks out? And anyway, a page full of huge headlines gets boring." Instead, designers set up a hierarchy of headlines to tell you how important a story is. "Developing a headline is an extraordinarily developed skill," continues Dr. Luskin. "It's designed to catch your attention in passing and get you to focus to a higher level of interest. If you can get even a fragment of attention, then you have something. Then you simply use repetition." Studies have shown that to commit something to memory, you have to go over it on four separate occasions. It works the same with print media. The more you read of a genre, the more familiar you get with it, and the easier it is to read. In fact, familiarity is one of the strongest weapons newspaper designers can wield. "We have a whole vocabulary of headlines that we understand and that we hope our reader understands subliminally," says Tom Bodkin, chief designer at the *New York Times*. "If you read the paper for any length of time, you get a feeling for what's important based on the style of the headline, the position on the page, all those little clues. It's a very complex language." Columns help to order the information. There's a lot to cram in, after all: The entire script of a half-hour TV news bulletin would fit on one page of a broadsheet newspaper. And color makes it more attractive. "Readers told us they like color on a page," says Pegie Stark Adam, "because they felt the pages with color on them had the most information, and they read more. Actually, when you study the tapes, they didn't read more, they just imagined they read more because of the color, which was really interesting." [Or was it? Did you read those 54 words without skipping any?]. Devices such as paragraphs, subheads and indents are meant to ease your reading, breaking up the article and encouraging the reader's attention to stay focused. [There should be a new paragraph here, for example]. So why do some people read newspapers that look boring, but don't read magazines that look exciting? The real secret of why you're still reading this story is CONTENT. "Design is about content, all the way along," says Ally Palmer of *The European*. "If you don't have content, you have nothing." The aim of media is to make the shift from peripheral attention (when you notice something in passing) to focused attention (when you stop and read or look at it). The surest, 100-percent foolproof way of doing that is to offer readers something that interests them. The Poynter Institute study discovered that people generally only read 25 percent of a newspaper. One of the stories the test group read contained no pictures, no subheads, and no color. In short, none of the usual devices. But 95 percent of people read it from start to finish. Why? It was about the difficulties of finding a baby-sitter. So if you've got this far, it's because you wanted to. And now, back to the design tricks.

76 COLORS

Atme tief durch. Auf dieser Seite stehen 1296 Wörter. Eigentlich sind das nicht so viele wie in einem normalen COLORS-Artikel. Nur, diesmal haben wir nichts getan, um dir Lust aufs Lesen zu machen. Hier gibt's keine kurzen Titel. Keine großen Photos. Keine bunten Farben. Tatsächlich stehen die Chancen, daß du bis ganz unten durchliest, gleich null. Du bist auch biologisch gar nicht dazu angelegt. "Menschen sind zum Lesen zu unterentwickelt," erklärt der Psychologe Arnold Wilkins von der Universität Essex, GB, der sich mit visuellen Aspekten beschäftigt. "Wir benutzen unsere zwei Augen, um Werkzeug zu ergreifen, aber Lesen ist kein natürlicher Vorgang - Texte existieren noch nicht lange genug." Der Mensch ist an landschaftliche Elemente gewöhnt, z.B. Bäume, oder den Anblick des Horizonts, die jede Menge natürliche Hinweise enthalten, an denen sich das Gehirn orientieren kann. Die Experten bezeichnen das als räumliche Differenzierungsfähigkeit: Wenn du deine Umgebung betrachtest, kannst du einen bestimmten Zweig vielleicht an der Art ausmachen, wie er am Baum sitzt, oder wie er sich von anderen Zweigen unterscheidet. [Herzlichen Glückwunsch, wenn du tatsächlich bis hier vorgedrungen bist. Die meisten Leute haben eine **Aufmerksamkeitsspanne von nur acht Sekunden.**] Im Gegensatz dazu hebt sich Text nicht sonderlich ab - er sieht fast immer gleich aus. Nichts an ihm zieht deine Aufmerksamkeit auf sich. Wenn du einen Text liest, hüpft dein rechtes Auge die Zeile entlang und landet dabei auf dem mittleren Drittel jedes Wortes. Das linke folgt ihm auf dem Fuße. Beide zusammen nehmen die weiteren zwei Drittel des Wortes wahr, bevor sie zum nächsten übergehen. Manchmal überspringen sie eins und müssen zurück überspringen sie eins und müssen zurück. Im großen und ganzen ist Lesen kein leichtes Unternehmen. Dann ist da noch die Anordnung des Textes. Von weitem sehen die horizontalen Textzeilen wie Striche aus. Du merkst es wahrscheinlich nicht, aber für deine Augen flimmert "gestreifter" Text (wie der in Büchern) und wird zum weiteren Streßfaktor für den Leser. Abgesehen davon, warum solltest du gerade diesen Artikel lesen? Tausend andere Dinge versuchen, deine Aufmerksamkeit auf sich zu ziehen: Die Gesamtmenge aller Druckerzeugnisse verdoppelt sich alle acht Jahre. Am 13. November 1987 umfaßte die *New York Times* 1612 Seiten, 12 Millionen Wörter und wog 5,4 kg - das Gewicht eines gesunden neugeborenen Zwillingspärchen. Es geht auch nicht nur um Gedrucktes: "An der Geschichte, daß Menschen auf Geräusche und visuelle Elemente geprägt sind, ist was dran," sagt Arnold Wilkins. "Informationen werden in mundgerechten Bissen angeboten, deshalb ist man gar nicht darauf angewiesen, sich lange konzentrieren zu können." In den 60er Jahren bestand ein einminütiger TV-Werbespot aus acht bis 12 Kameraeinstellungen. Ein Spot jüngeren Herstellungsdatums, der jungen Leuten Lust auf ein Erfrischungsgetränk machen soll, hat 22 Einstellungen in 30 Sekunden - das ist ca. ein Bild pro Sekunde. Der durchschnittliche Fernsehzuschauer schaltet per Fernbedienung pro Stunde 35mal auf einen anderen Kanal um. Kein Wunder, daß Werbeleute wissen, daß Sätze mit mehr als vier Worten nicht funktionieren, meint der amerikanische Medienpsychologe Dr. Bernard Luskin. (*"Just do it!"* - Tu's doch!) Das heißt: Noch bevor du anfängst, diesen Artikel zu lesen, stehen die Chancen, daß du bist zum Ende durchhälst, gleich null, weil es Unmengen anderer Dinge gibt, die dich ablenken. Deshalb wird bei Zeitungen und Zeitschriften alles getan, um dein Interesse zu fesseln. Wichtig ist, zu wissen, wie du liest. Pegie Stark Adam erstellte vor ein paar Jahren eine diesbezügliche Studie für das Poynter-Institut für Medienwissenschaften in Florida, USA. "Wir verfolgten mit zwei winzigen Kameras genau, wie sich die Augen der Versuchspersonen über die Seite bewegten, registrierten, woran der Blick wie lange hängenblieb, wo er zuerst hinfiel, wo an zweiter Stelle, an dritter, an vierter, und so fort," erklärt sie. 95% der Leser sehen sich zuerst die Photos an. Das überrascht Arnold Wilkins mitnichten. "Wie bei den Naturlandschaften variiert der räumliche Inhalt der Photos mit seiner räumlichen Anordnung." Selbst wenn du einen Universitätsabschluß hast, ist wahrscheinlich, daß du [644 Wörter - du hast die erste Hälfte überstanden] nur ein Fünftel des Vokabulars deiner Muttersprache tatsächlich beherrschst. Daher übersetzen wir hier das Zitat von Professor Wilkins: "Photos sind abwechslungsreicher als Text." Deshalb ist die in ihnen enthaltene Information leichter zu verstehen. Nach den Photos liest du vielleicht die Untertitel, aber deine Augen streben wahrscheinlich zurück zur Schlagzeile. Je größer, desto besser? Nicht unbedingt. Halte diese Seite etwas von dir weg. Das, was du von weitem erkennen kannst, zieht deinen Blick auf sich, wenn er über die Seite gleitet. Fettgedruckter Text erregt mehr Interesse als Text in großen Lettern, obwohl es nützlich ist, ein paar Titel mit auf die Seite zu setzen: "Wenn du jetzt schon täglich eine riesige Schlagzeile hast, was machst du dann, wenn der dritte Weltkrieg ausbricht?" fragt Simon Esterson vom britischen Guardian. "Außerdem ist eine Seite voller Riesentitel langweilig." Statt dessen gibt es eine regelrechte Rangordnung für Schlagzeilen, aus der man erkennen kann, wie wichtig ein Artikel ist. "Hinter einem Titel steckt jede Menge Arbeit am Detail," fährt Dr. Luskin fort. "Er soll deine Aufmerksamkeit erhaschen und dein Interesse wecken. Selbst ein winziger Teil Aufmerksamkeit ist schon etwas. Danach wird einfach wiederholt." Studien zufolge muß etwas, das im Gedächtnis hängenbleiben soll, bei vier verschiedenen Gelegenheiten wahrgenommen werden. Das gleiche gilt für Gedrucktes. Je öfter du eine bestimmte Zeitung oder Zeitschrift liest, desto besser ist sie dir bekannt und desto leichter fällt dir das Lesen. Der Bekanntheitsgrad wird daher zu einer der stärksten Waffen der Zeitungsgrafiker. "Wir haben ein richtiggehendes Vokabular für unsere Titel, daß wir verstehen und von dem wir hoffen, daß es auch unseren Lesern unbewußt geläufig ist," sagt Tom Bodkin, Verantwortlicher für Design bei der *New York Times*. "Wer die Zeitung regelmäßig liest, bekommt ein Gefühl dafür, was uns wichtig ist: an der Art der Schlagzeile, der Position des Artikels auf der Seite, solche Details eben. Das ist eine sehr komplexe Art der Kommunikation." Die Anordnung in Spalten trägt dazu bei, die Informationsmasse zu ordnen, und das ist nicht wenig: Eine halbstündige TV-Nachrichtensendung würde auf die Seite einer Zeitung herkömmlichen Formats passen. Farben machen das Ganze attraktiver: "Die Leser mögen farbige Seiten," sagt Pegie Stark Adam, "sie haben das Gefühl, farbige Seiten beinhalten mehr Information, und sie lesen mehr davon. Wenn man das allerdings genauer untersucht, kommt heraus, daß sie gar nicht mehr lesen, sie glauben nur, mehr gelesen zu haben, wegen der Farbe, die wirklich interessant war." [Oder nicht? Hast du diese 58 Wörter gelesen, ohne eins zu überspringen?]. Andere Textmittel wie Absätze, Untertitel und Einzüge sollen dir das Lesen erleichtern, indem sie den Artikel unterteilen und das ungeteilte Interesse des Lesers behalten. [Hier zum Beispiel könnte ein neuer Absatz anfangen]. Warum lesen dann so viele Leute Zeitungen, die eher langweilig aussehen, und nicht ausschließlich Magazine, die interessant und aufregend erscheinen? Das Geheimnis dieses Artikels, der wahre Grund, aus dem du immer noch liest, ist sein INHALT. "Grafik hat immer etwas mit dem Inhalt zu tun," erklärt Ally Palmer vom "European". "Wenn der Inhalt nichts hergibt, kann man mit Design auch nicht viel machen." Das Ziel der Medien ist, generelle Aufmerksamkeit (mit der etwas im Vorbeigehen beachtet wird) zu gezielter Aufmerksamkeit (die dich dazu bringt, stehen zu bleiben und etwas zu lesen oder anzusehen) zu machen. Die 100%ig sicherste Art, das zu schaffen, ist, dem Leser etwas anzubieten, was ihn interessiert. Die Studie des Poynter-Instituts zeigt, daß meistens nur 25% einer Zeitung gelesen wird. Einer der Texte, der den Testlesern vorgelegt wurde, enthielt weder Photos noch Untertitel noch Farbe - kurz, keines der herkömmlichen Mittel. Trotzdem lasen 95% der Testpersonen den Text vom ersten bis zum letzten Wort. Warum? In dem Text ging es um die Schwierigkeiten bei der Suche nach einem Babysitter. Wenn du also diesen Artikel bis hier gelesen hast, hast du das getan, weil du ihn lesen wolltest. Und jetzt geht's weiter mit den Grafiktricks.

COLORS 77

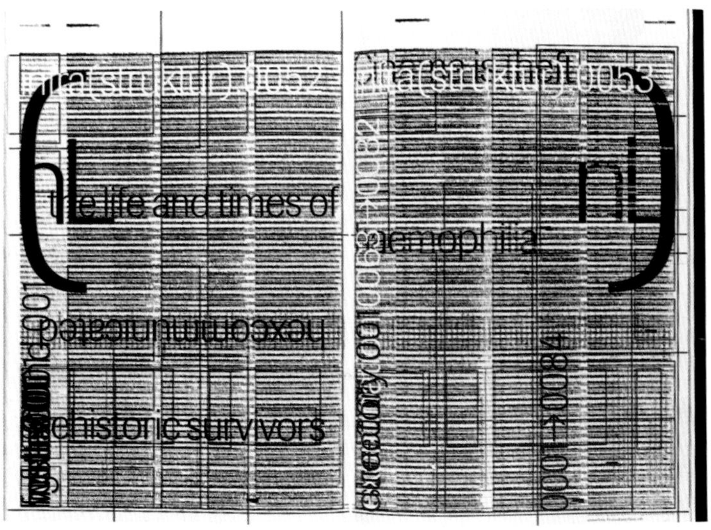

Most editorial designers rely on a modest range of typographic 'tricks' to break up the text and inject pace and energy into the layout without confusing the reader or distracting their attention from what is really important – the content itself. Many of these techniques are comparatively obvious: putting headlines and standfirsts in large or bold type, and placing them where the reader would expect an article to start – in the top left hand corner of a left hand page, for example. More subtle methods regularly employed by magazine designers include the use of an outsize initial at the start of the text (common practice since monks first hand-lettered Bibles), indents for quotations from other texts, line breaks for reported speech, a one-line space between paragraphs, or other features such as a series of dots or stars to identify a natural break in the text.

The Observer newspaper's magazine supplement, Life, employs several of these typographic techniques to great effect: in the example shown here, the title is set in extremely large type, which varies in colour to highlight both the subject of the article, Pakistani politician Imran Khan, and the interesting interplay between the shape of the words 'no' and 'do'. The names of the writer and photographer are picked out in bold; the sans serif standfirst stands out because of its size and its positioning in a sea of white space, while the outsize sans serif initial attracts the reader's eye to the start of the article itself, set in a four column grid (two of which are taken up by the image). On the second spread, an imposing sans serif pull quote, spaces between paragraphs and the highlighting in bold of the first line after each break makes the layout not just stylish, but manageable.

Furthermore, this easy readability has been achieved without sacrificing dignity and gravitas: this is, after all, the UK's oldest Sunday newspaper, and one whose diverse readership requires it to run interviews with pop stars and actors next to accounts of injustice, war, and other less frivious topics. Other magazines, particularly those aimed at a youth audience, are freer to cast off the shackles of quiet restraint: as Mark Porter observes, impenetrability in these cases is almost regarded as a badge of honour, 'which is why you end up with heavy metal magazines where people are prepared to read articles in black letter type reversed out of a photograph. In most cases people just wouldn't bother. They'd try to read two or three words and just forget about it. But your 16-year-old heavy metal fiend is so desperate to find out about his Brazilian heavy metal band that he's prepared to make the effort, and the fact that it's hard to read makes it kind of personal, in the same way that teenagers love the fact that parents hate the music they listen to.'

A 10ft-long poster of Imran Khan at the Mochi Gate rally in Lahore, March 1999. Despite the adulation, the opposition is dismissive. 'The people don't love Khan the way they love me,' states Benazir Bhutto.

Words **Jason Burke** Photographs **Karen Davies**

No Khan do

Once a playboy cricketer, Imran Khan is now a campaigning politician. He has his fans, but most see him as a figure of fun. He has no chance of election. So what makes Imran run?

I is a warm spring evening in the busy eastern Pakistani city of Lahore. The sun slants through thick clouds of exhaust and dust, and flickers off the mirrors of the milling rickshaws, and catches the gaudy, polished foil decorations on the pony traps and buses. Crowds of workers interrupt their journeys home to gather around the kebab stands and the men who sell fresh juice for a few rupees. Veiled women soundlessly pass through the tumult like ghosts.

Halfway round the Circular Road that girdles central Lahore with a ribbon of noise and pollution is the Mochi Gate. Once a gap in the wall that the Mughal emperors built around their town, it is now a football-pitch-sized patch of dust and gravel, with a podium flanked by concrete terraces and a huge, rusting hoarding. Strung from the hoarding are banners covered in Urdu script and two giant, luridly painted portraits. One is of Jinnah, the founder of Pakistan; the other is of Imran Khan, former cricketer, playboy and now campaigning politician.

This evening, the ground in front of the podium is a mass of babbling, shouting, grinning men. Many wear the green and red of Khan's party, the Tehrik-e-Insaaf (Movement for Justice). There are 4,000 of them, and more are still arriving. The loudspeakers spit out the names of their home towns through a shower of static: Multan, Sahiwal, Sargodha, Rawalpindi, Shekhupura.

By 7pm, it is dark, and a dozen drums are keeping up a steady rhythm around the ground. When Khan arrives, the crowd erupts. *Kaun pauncheage Pakistan?* (Who will save Pakistan?) is screamed through the loudspeakers, and 5,000 men hoarsely bellow, 'Imran Khaaan, Imran Khaaan, Imran Khaaan', holding the second name until they run out of breath. The fireworks spatter colour across Lahore's night sky, the drums thud and rattle, and the crowd's roar deepens and thickens and grows.

But when, after nervously smoothing his hair, Khan raises his hands – palms forwards, arms straight – they are silent. And for the next 40 minutes, as his rich, bass voice rolls through the crackling speakers and out across a 100m-deep sea of expectant, overexcited faces, there is quiet. As he speaks, Khan holds a rolled sheaf of notes scribbled in his left hand. At the top of the first page is written in red pen, in his ▶

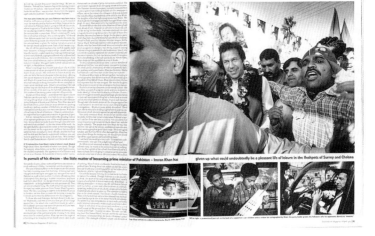

In pursuit of his dream – the little matter of becoming prime minister of Pakistan

given up what could undoubtedly be a pleasant life of leisure in the fleshpots of Surrey and Chelsea

Debates about readability, particularly in relation to magazines, have raged throughout the 1990s, inspired in part by the work of David Carson on magazines such as *Ray Gun*. Carson argues with some justification that to their target audience, his magazines are perfectly legible. The opposing camp argues that design should be an invisible presence in a layout, existing only to allow the reader to interpret the words and images on the page as easily as possible. Like most debates of this nature, there is no clear-cut solution. What the arguments do show quite clearly, though, is that there are a wide range of reading constituencies consuming magazines, and that the arrangement of information within them is critical in determining the way in which they are received. Between *The Economist*, on the one hand, whose unobtrusive and formalised layout is designed simply to impart as much complex information as quickly as possible to the reader, and *Ray Gun* or *Straight no Chaser* on the other, which make a feature out of design in the same way as they do photography and writing, lie most magazines.

In his Thames & Hudson *Manual of Typography*, the writer and typographer Ruari McLean suggests that 'there is normally a strong argument in favour of a standard "pattern": people who look at a magazine regularly (whether they buy it, borrow it, or get it pushed through their letterbox) want to recognise it as they do a friend; they want the layout to be familiar.' The typographic styling of a magazine identifies it to the reader; it subconsciously tells them where they are in the magazine (wide columns, bold headlines and serif type, then you're in the features section; narrower columns, and sans serif type, and it's listings, for example). But it does more than this: in a way that few readers would consciously recognise, the typographic framework of a magazine is the skeleton on which the flesh of layouts are built, and in that respect perhaps more fundamental to the visual character of a magazine than covers, illustrations or a skilfully executed pagination combined.

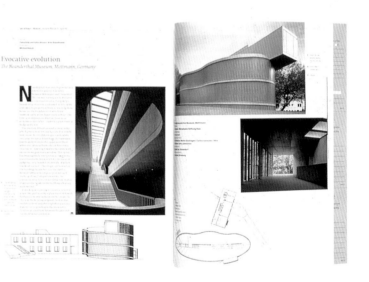

BIG VOICE

WHEN SHE FIRST SANG IN TEXAS, SHARLEEN SPITERI RESEMBLED A VERTICALLY CHALLENGED TOMBOY. HOW DID THE SHORT SCOT WITH THE BROKEN NOSE BECOME A SEX SYMBOL? INTERVIEW BY DYLAN JONES. PHOTOGRAPHS BY CRAIG McDEAN

Eye
Issue: 4, 1991
Art director:
Stephen Coates
UK

Neue Graphik
Issue: 2/1959
Art directors:
Richard P. Lohse
J. Müller-Brockmann
Hans Neuberg
Carlo L. Vivarelli
Switzerland

Eye
Issue: 4, 1991
Art director:
Stephen Coates
UK

World Architecture
Issue: Apr 1997
Art director:
Struktur Design
UK

Van
Issue: Oct 1998
Art director:
Fernando Gutiérrez
Spain

**Sunday Times
Magazine**
issue: Mar 1999
Art director:
Andrew McConochie
UK

SUEÑOS
DE
GLORIA

LOS TOROS. LA LOCURA DE UN PAÍS, LA LOCURA DE LA PLAZA, LA LOCURA DE LOS
TOROS. LA METÁFORA DE UN PUEBLO QUE HA CONVERTIDO EL RITO DEL TOREO EN
UN DOCUMENTO DE IDENTIDAD. LOS RASTROS DE UNA OBSESIÓN QUE EMPIEZA
TOREANDO AL AIRE. fotografía GIORGIA FIORIO

Hårt/mjukt, spetsigt/runt,
öppet/slutet: detaljer med
dubbla budskap.

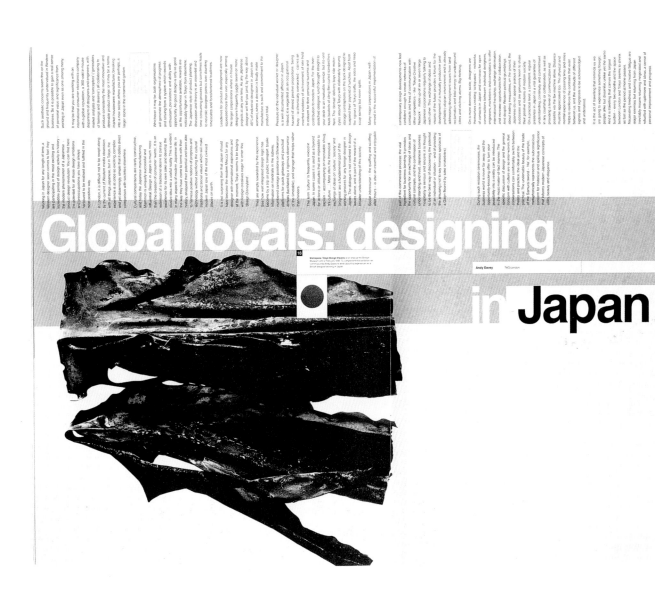

Global locals: designing in Japan

Andy Davey   T&G London

Bibel
Issue: Jan 1999
Art director:
Stefania Malmsten
Sweden

Matador
Issue: 'CH', 1999
Art director:
Fernando Gutiérrez
Spain

Issue
Issue: 8, 1991
Art director:
Cartlidge Levene
UK

Rhythmus

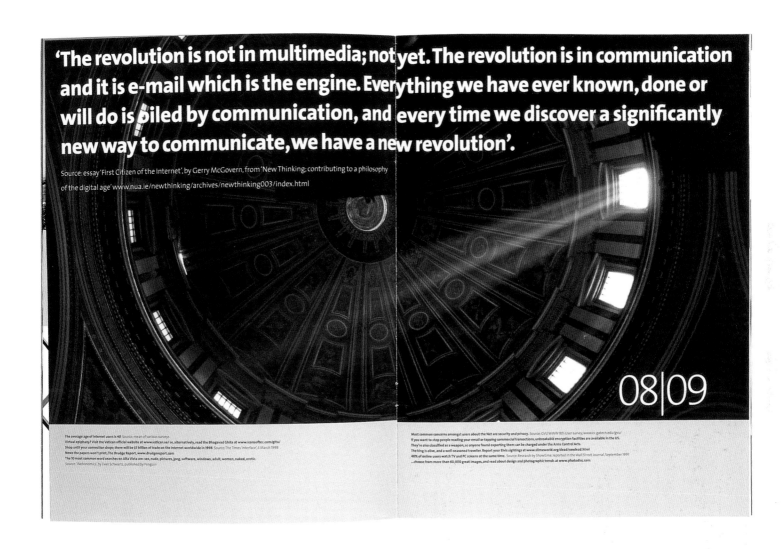

Form & Zweck
Issue: 2/3, 1991
Art director: cyan
Germany

Form & Zweck
Issue: 4/5, 1992
Art director: cyan
Germany

Typographische
Monatsblätter
Issue: 4, 1959
Switzerland

dFusion
Issue: 1, 1998
Art director:
Struktur Design
UK

Captions

If all design is about the interplay between text and pictures, then this is seen particularly clearly in magazine design. In consumer magazines at least, the two usually enjoy equal weight, so that one might say that a magazine, unlike a newspaper perhaps, is as much about image as it is about words. In some instances text supports the image, in some instances image is there to support the text. But the two must always, to a greater or lesser extent, work together. The way that this happens can be seen in microcosm in the case of captions, which might be seen as the literal and metaphorical bridge between text and image.

Captions themselves can work in a number of ways and have several different functions: captions, can be, for instance, an information-driven page map, supplementary information, relating to a specific image (as in the cases of *Azure* and *Cover*), or supplementary information to the bulk of the text: the example reproduced here from *Baseline* magazine, for example, contains substantial amounts of information about the subject of the article that is not included in the body copy, and does not relate to any specific image.

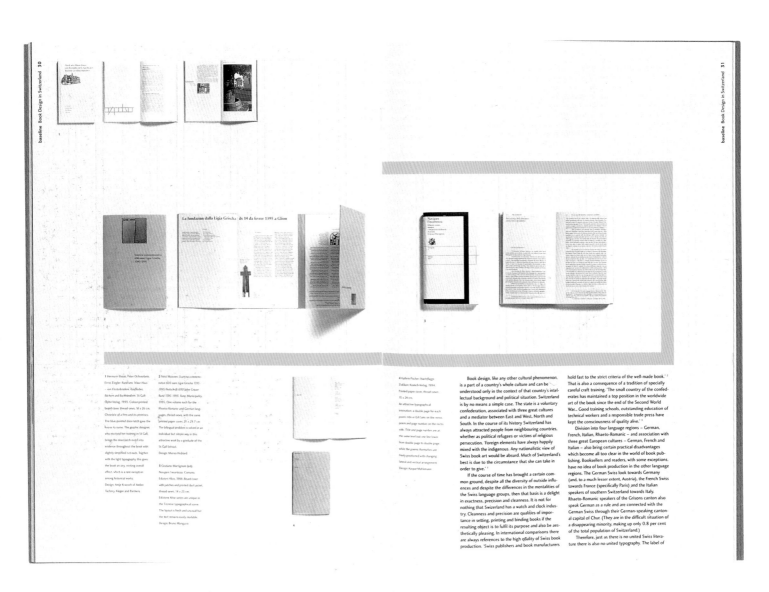

Baseline
Issue: 22, 1996
Art direction:
hdr Design
UK

Graphics
International
Issue: 57, Jul 1998
Design:
Andy Jennings
UK

Azure
issue: Nov/Dec 1998
Art director:
Concrete Design
Communications
Canada

Cover
Issue: Mar 1999
Art director:
Samantha Harrison
UK

One of the most important elements of caption design is the establishment of a device which clearly identifies which caption applies to what. At the most simple level, this is often achieved by positioning the caption directly alongside or beneath the image to which it relates. If the designer believes the reader will be sufficiently motivated to navigate a more complex mechanism, however, or if, for example, there is simply no room on the page next to the image, or the captions are very long, a more complex system may be instituted. In the case of *Graphics International*, a caption map is drawn with numbers which are arranged in direct proportion to the position of the images on the page, reading from the top left hand side of the page down. Next to the diagram sit the captions, identified by corresponding numbers. *Baseline*, on the other hand, positions the numbers next to the images themselves, while grouping the actual captions unobtrusively on the margins of the page.

The
art of
Sculpture

is a creative approach to problem solving, combined with a wide range of skills & capabilities

```
1     2
           3      3 | Part of Alan Kitching's
      4                 collection of wood
                        letter, in use at the
1 | 'In Darkest England',    Typography Workshop
    designed by David Jury
2 | 'The Art of Sculpture',   4 | The Art of Sculpture',
                                 designed by David Jury
```

designed by David Jury

House of Naylor
+44 (0)171 404 6555

The Typography
Workshop
+44 (0)171 490 4386

GROUND FLOOR

MEZZANINE

Nettwerk textByAdeleWeder

(LEFT AND CENTRE) THE HEAVY TIMBER, DOUGLAS FIR FURNITURE IN THE LOUNGE AND THROUGHOUT THE PROJECT WAS MADE OF OFF-CUTS FROM RESIZING THE EXIST-ING CEILING BEAMS. (RIGHT) THE 'WALLS OF SHAME' ARE ANOTHER EXAMPLE OF CREATIVE RECYCLING. THE UNDULATING WALL SECTION IS ACTUALLY COMPOSED – FLOOR TO CEILING – OF UNSOLD CDS. (TOP) NETTWERK'S SPLASHY FRONT FOYER OPENS INTO THE LOUNGE TO MAKE ONE LONG PARTY SPACE FOR CD LAUNCHES.

breakfast every day of his life. And even at 90 he could drink more beer than I could.

Most of them were still taking a drink or two. When I went to see Daly Briscoe, a retired Suffolk GP, he took me out to the pub for lunch where we went through the menu and drank wine. Emma Logan in Manchester was still having a Guinness a day. The Queen Mum, so we are led to believe, is still fond of a tipple.

You can take it to excess and still survive. Leonard Cooper, ex-Radley and Oxford, father of Leo Cooper the publisher (and father-in-law of Jilly), did take drink to excess in his thirties and forties, but when I saw him at his daughter's home in Norfolk he was sparkling. Not having had a drink for 39 years had obviously given his liver a chance to recover.

Having a routine and living an ordered life would seem to be valuable. All of them, even those in the humblest of occupations, had always been organised. Dur-

In 1900, some 60,000 people in the UK reached the age of 85. By 2000, there will be 1,158,000 people in the UK over the age of 85. Being old will be nothing out of the ordinary

Top: Leonard Vale-Onslow, the world's oldest motorcyclist with a valid licence, and, left, aged four with his sister Enid. Above: Mary Ellis today and, left, in the 1935 Hollywood film *All the King's Horses*

ing the long years of retirement, they had created frameworks and rituals.

But the thing that struck me most about them all was their outgoingness. Even at the age of 97 and 98, and not necessarily in the best of health, they were not self-obsessed. They were interested in other people, and always had been, according to their children. They were still curious. If you want to live to a ripe old age, acquire the art of looking out at the world, not in at yourself.

The Guardian

Born 1900 is available for £13.99 plus 99p P&P, (RRP £16.99) from the Cover Bookshop (0181 324 5573)

cover magazine *March 1999*

139

Images

Interview
with Stephen Gan
Picture treatment
Illustration

**Interview
with Stephen Gan**

There comes a time in the career of many an art director when, having exhausted the possibilities offered by existing magazines, the only way to do work that satisfies is to start their own publication. For Stephen Gan, publisher and art director of *Visionaire*, it happened comparatively early on, but then Gan's career got off to a flying start when, aged just 20, he became fashion editor of *Details*, then a 'down-town, underground magazine' in the New York of the early 1980s.

Gan had originally set out to be a fashion photographer, studying the subject at college alongside elements of communication design, but having got the job on *Details*, he realised that magazines were a forum in which he could indulge several passions simultaneously: 'When I started working on a magazine, I found that I enjoyed that, and I was able to combine my love for photography with being an editor,' he explains. 'There was that side to things – putting a story together – that I enjoyed. I loved not only the photography but making sure that it was laid out well and looking good within the overall format of the magazine.'

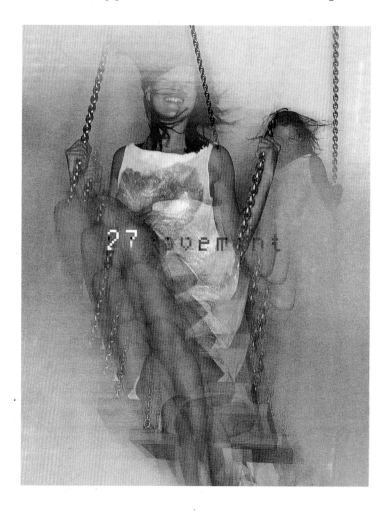

**Cover of
Visionaire 27
'Movement'**

**Visionaire 20
'Commes des
Garçons'**

**Cover of
Visionaire 25
'Visionary'**

Gan's tenure at *Details* came to an end at the close of the '80s, when the magazine temporarily disbanded. Having developed his own interests and talents within the parameters of that magazine, which was among the most radical in fashion publishing, Gan realised that there was nowhere else that he could work that would allow him to explore all of his enthusiasms fully: 'I was left with the love of all these things but not wanting to work anywhere as one particular thing. I would be working as a photographer or as an art director or a fashion editor, but I wanted to do all of those things, so I had no choice but to start my own magazine. I spoke to a few other people and they said "You can't work for anyone else, you have to start one of your own",' he recollects now.

The magazine he founded was *Visionaire*, which came into being in 1991. From its outset it was a team effort as Gan entered into partnership with two friends, Cecilia Dean, a model, and James Kaliardos, a make-up artist. Its beginnings were, in a sense, inauspicious: Gan, as a former fashion editor, had the most magazine experience, although the others had been peripherally involved with magazines through their work – but none had ever published a magazine before; furthermore, there was no precedent for a magazine like *Visionaire*, and the team did not feel that they had identified a gap in the market, an opportunity ripe for exploitation, but rather 'We looked at the other magazines that were out there and said "What do we feel is lacking? What do we feel like adding?" And that was a very personal viewpoint – we wanted to do something that looked like a personal portfolio of favourite images.'

In terms of its content, too, the early *Visionaire* was essentially uncommercial: that is not a judgement on the quality of the work, but reflects a conscious decision on the part of its publishers: 'We knew a lot of artists – photographers and illustrators – who we had either worked with or were friends with, and it was just a way to publish their personal work, which didn't seem to get published a lot. We found that whoever we met seemed to have personal images stashed away in a drawer that they were really proud of, but were never seen by anyone because their published shoots were all for commercial magazines.' From its earliest days, *Visionaire* has been built on the twin foundations of enthusiasm and experimentation – if it sounded interesting, they'd give it a go.

Today, according to Gan, '99 per cent' of the work featured in *Visionaire* is commissioned by the magazine, for the magazine, but many of the contributors are the same and the basis of friendship and trust between the publishers of the magazine and its artists remains: indeed, that relationship, and the confidence it inspires, is the basis of the ongoing commitment of the magazine to experimentation and 'discussion'. 'We're quite selective in the way we choose our artists,' says Gan, 'but when you get a certain roster of people you trust, I think it's important to give them freedom. Somebody once called *Visionaire* "a gallery in print" – it's a very apt description, I think. We come up with these group shows: "This is the theme we chose, and this is what our artists came up with."'

Visionaire has also stayed true to its roots in that it thrives on the collaborative creative process. When describing it, Gan uses phrases such as 'brainstorming session', 'creative lab' and even 'harmonic convergence'. Outside input has been brought to the process by the invitation to guest edit issues, extended to designers such as Karl Lagerfeld and Comme des Garçons, as well as the multifarious talents on that roster of artists. 'With magazines, it's all about collaboration,' says Gan, giving as 'a prime example of how important collaboration is to Visionaire' the cover of issue 27, 'Movement'. The cover itself is made of a lenticular material so that as it is moved, the model appears to swing back and forth. It is the product of creative input from some of the top names in several different fields: the fashion designer Alexander McQueen came to the shoot to style the dress on to the model, Kate Moss; the photographer Nick Knight took the picture, which was conceived by the graphic designer Peter Saville. The technical know-how was provided by Chris Levine, a leading expert in laser and holographic techniques.

The animated cover is one of a number of ways in which Visionaire has not only pushed the envelope of editorial design, but blown it right open. Other issues have assumed the form of a pack of playing cards, a Luis Vuitton handbag, a round wooden box and a metal tin. The decision to change the format with every issue was made before the publication of issue one, and as Gan explains, there is a genuine benefit in doing so: 'In order for our artists to get excited about an issue, it's important to excite ourselves first, to say "What haven't we done yet?" An extreme example of that is the Gucci lightbox, which we did with [Gucci's creative director] Tom Ford. There we really struggled with production, and we had to stick to our guns and remind ourselves that we were going through these electronic and technological difficulties because we had set that challenge for ourselves. We had given ourselves this task of always trying something new – it's very much a part of what we do.'

Visionaire 23
'The Emperor's
New Clothes'
edited by Karl
Lagerfeld

Cover of
Visionaire 8
'The Orient'

Cover of
Visionaire 14
'Hype'

Visionaire 26
'Fantasy'

The fact that *Visionaire* is so closely associated with the three-dimensional means that it could never successfully make the transition to the web (although its current site, which Gan describes as a 'billboard' for the magazine, is among the most attractive and forward-looking on the web at the time of writing, seamlessly integrating flawless graphics, animation and music). A proposed spin off from *Visionaire* – a mass-market print fashion magazine entitled *V* – will, however, be mirrored by an on-line version. And while it may spawn big-selling, advertising-friendly relatives, *Visionaire* itself will never be available to a mass market – its fate in that regard was determined on the day the publishers decided to change the format with each issue, reject advertising and with it the constraints imposed on commercial magazine publishing: 'It wasn't meant to be exclusive,' explains Gan, 'but it was meant to be limited. It has become exclusive because it's become very expensive, because we've had to out-do ourselves with every issue.'

So it's a magazine of which only a few thousand copies of any issue will be printed, is more likely to come in the form of a lightbox or a handbag as a bound piece of print, contains almost no words and costs twice as much as the average art book. One might argue that it is only in the sense that each issue is a collection with a theme or definition that it is a magazine at all: 'Exactly,' confirms Gan. 'In fact, we tend not to use the term magazine. Everyone who writes on it calls it the hippest, or the most exclusive, or the most expensive magazine in the world, but we don't really see it as a magazine.' So what is it? 'A publication. In the beginning we used to refer to it as "a multi-format album of inspiration", but that's too long. A lot of people also refer to it as "that thing".' he laughs.

While it may be hard – or even impossible – to define, the success and appeal of *Visionaire* have brought plenty of outside commissions through the doors of the building in SoHo, New York, occupied by Gan, his partners, and the six designers who make up the publishers' studio. They art direct on average two advertising campaigns a year for clients such as Calvin Klein, and in 1999 have designed two books, *Fashion 2001* and fashion photographer and *Visionaire* regular Mario Testino's latest, *Front Row, Back Stage*. *Visionaire* itself sells out every issue, and certain back numbers change hands for thousands of dollars. In retrospect, Stephen Gan may well feel that the decision taken nearly a decade ago not to settle for second best, but to launch a new magazine that would not only make the best use of his various talents, but that would uncompromisingly reflect the tastes, influences, interests and concerns of his friends, was the right one to make.

In the mid 1960s, a young photojournalist named Don McCullin made his name with a series of evocative and powerful images of the war in Vietnam. Simultaneously, the magazine in which they were published, *The Sunday Times Magazine*, already notable for its use of colour images, became associated with the photo-story, and the developing genre of photojournalism. It's an association the magazine maintains to this day. By devoting several consecutive spreads to photographs, each allocated a generous space and accompanied only by brief captions, *The Sunday Times Magazine* introduced a generation of readers to the concept that stories told in pictures were not just for children.

Readers were, of course, already familiar with the visual narrative in other contexts: fashion magazines have been running predominantly visual features for as long as there have been fashion magazines. In those publications, a series of spreads showing models in swimwear, or evening wear, constitutes a feature as surely as 2,000 closely argued words on command economies does in a political weekly. Today, that format is used not just for clothes, but for interiors, food, consumer durables and any number of other products which are of interest as much for the way they look as anything words can say about them. Perhaps the most extreme example of the photo-story is to be found in issue 13 of *Colors* magazine. Its editor-in-chief, the late Tibor Kalman, borrowed an idea from 'Powers of Ten', a film by the American furniture designers Charles and Ray Eames. Over the course of the issue the reader observes the world from an increasingly shrunken perspective: from a global overview, shot from space to a microscopic look at life on earth. The issue contained no words whatsoever, but had a powerful sense of narrative.

BEYOND BELIEF

They are raped, enslaved, falsely accused, beaten to death and have their homes bulldozed. Their only crime: to be Christians in Pakistan. Cathy Scott-Clark and Adrian Levy investigate. Photographs by Harriet Logan

Her mother was the only one to hear the story. The seven-year-old whispered it once and since then has hardly talked at all. She was returning from a friend's house at 11.30am, when someone called out. As she turned, four men from her village ran towards her. Nageena ran too, tripping on her scarf, stumbling on the unmade road. She is not sure why she ran – because they were running, because they had never spoken to her before, because the only man she had ever talked to was her father. But the four men were faster, cornering her, catching her. She could remember being pushed through a wooden door and into a dark room, which smelt of damp sacking and grass. She screamed but could not describe what happened next.

Villagers heard her crying and a crowd gathered outside the *dera*, or cow shed. Ghulam Masih saw the commotion, ran over and pulled open the door. Inside he saw Alla, Ditta, Rashid and Javid, the sons of his neighbour, standing over his daughter, her clothes tangled with straw, her legs covered in blood. As he scooped Nageena into his arms, the four men backed away and ran across a rice field.

Ghulam and Shehnaz, his wife, carried their daughter to the police station, filed a criminal complaint and were put on the bus to Shekhupura hospital, in Pakistan's Punjab province. It was 10.30pm by the time they arrived, and Dr Zahida Noor was about to go home. "Hymen torn off, first-degree tear, fresh bleeding, a wound and tear marks on her right and left thigh, semen and blood stains taken from clothes," the medical report concluded. Dr Noor told Ghulam and Shehnaz that their daughter's internal injuries were so severe that she would never be able to have children.

Over the next two weeks, as Nageena hid under her hospital blanket, the Sharqpur police arrested Alla, Ditta, Rashid and Javid, after dozens of villagers came forward with their names. It would be another six weeks before Nageena would talk again to her mother, and when she did it was to ask why the four rapists were back in her village. Mushtaq Ahmed, inspector of police, had freed them and closed the case. He said he could find no evidence and told Nageena's family to forget the matter. But Ghulam continued to demand justice and refused gifts of a new home, money, sweets and clothes from the men who had raped his daughter.

Nineteen months later, the family thought his determination had paid off. They received a letter from a new government department, the Human Rights Ministry of Pakistan, which said it had reviewed the criminal file and decided to award Nageena £200 compensation. Two weeks later, Ghulam Masih was back at Sharqpur police station. This time he was lying half-naked with his face in the dirt, heavy ⇒→ 29

Ghulam Masih in a police cell in Sharqpur. The gang who raped his daughter, Nageena, when she was seven, have falsely accused him of murder

The Sunday Times Magazine
Issue: Jan 1999
Art director:
Andrew McConochie
Photographer:
Harriet Logan
UK

Blah Blah Blah
Issue: May 1996
Art director:
Substance
UK

View on Colour
Issue: 13,
1999–2000
Art directors:
Anthon Beeke,
Lidewij Edelkoort
France

But while, in the right circumstances, readers will read a story either entirely in words or one told in pictures, in the vast majority of instances the two work together in a range of ways that separate magazines from books and newspapers.

Subconsciously, the reader continually cross-references the text and the image, looking to one for insights into the other. For that reason, the positioning of images on the page is critical: the reader will automatically look to the image and back when the text seems to refer to it, and if the eye has to travel too far around the page, and gets lost on the way back to the text, the reader will find themselves disconcerted, frustrated and unsettled – an uncomfortable reading experience.

Commissioning photography, or sourcing it from photolibraries, is a job sometimes done by a picture editor, but one that usually falls to the art director. Each art director has their own way of working with photographers: some develop close working relationships that inform the look of the whole magazine, where the personal styles of the art director and photographer start to infuse that of the other. Some art directors are more off-hand, and do not feel the need to be present at shoots or discuss camera angles at length, trusting instead that the photographer they have commissioned will fulfil the brief, add a little something of their own and deliver a usable set of pictures. But either way, the art director must be clear about the way they want the magazine to work in advance – to know what they want photographed, by who and in what style, and how those pictures will work on the page – in order to preserve the coherence of the art director's overall vision for the publication.

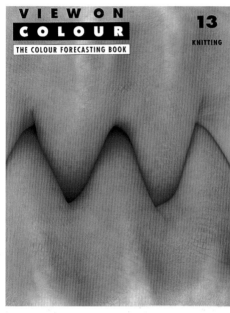

BLUNDERWALL

hese stars
lisc, (What's

Oh man, what you gotted best on the cover for?"
Noel Gallagher in blah blah blah's Damon Albarn cover.

nothing better to do: craig mclean likewise: joseph cultice

On their last weekend "Slutwalk" BLAH BLAH looks the catchman with...
"victory lap" hat gals distracted by a bunch of hardcore punk kids. Some might say, "Hey, who needs another Oasis interview anyway?

Die
geliebte
Frau

Auch so kann Katharina sein,
Gebht. – ein Begriff für den
Zustand der Seele und der
Haare. Die geliebte Frau. Für
den Mann, der hinaus muß
ins öffentliche Leben. Das
Beisammensein in eine andere
Realität. Diese Wirklichkeit
heißt nicht nur Erotik. Sie
heißt Stille, Traum, trachten-
de Ruhe, örtliche und ver-
schwülige Worte. Einmalige
und endlose Begegnung. Jeden Tag, jeden eine Jahr.
Vielleicht noch viele Jahre.
Vielleicht das große Los.

For the new European, style in the shopping
aisle is no
longer a five
letter swear word.

Just say non to sell-in-bulk shell suits and oui, merci to off-the-
shelf suits. Au revoir 2.2 screaming kids and a Renault Espace
in the car park, bonjour sunday socials by the vegetable racks.
Cucumbers were last year, honey, the choice of '96 is the
squash...

Sweep de HyperMarché

Mathieu

Zoe

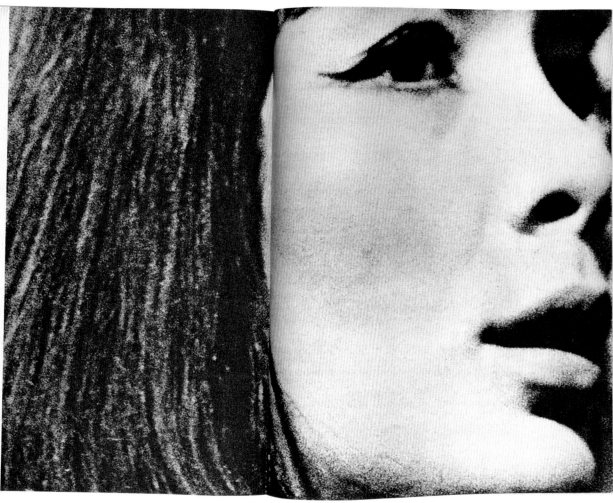

der vorsichtigste Mensch der Welt.
Er fuhr nie verrückte Geschwindig-
keiten und mißtraute den andern Auto-
fahrern, jenen, die nicht Herr über ihre
Reflexe sind. Von sich selber wußte
er, daß er auch noch bei 250 Stunden-
kilometern die absolute Herrschaft
über sein Fahrzeug haben würde. Es
sind jene „andern" gewesen, die un-
absichtlich schuld an seinem Tode
geworden sind. Eine Handvoll Neu-
gieriger, fanatischer Anhänger von
Automobilrennen, lief über die Renn-
bahn. In diesem Augenblick kam
Jean-Pierre mit Höchstgeschwindig-
keit heran. Er hatte nur einen knappen
Augenblick der Wahl: er oder die
andern. Er wählte sich selbst.

86

Blah Blah Blah
Issue: May 1996
Art director:
Substance
UK

Blah Blah Blah
Issue: May 1996
Art director:
Substance
UK

Twen
Issue date: 1962
Art director:
Willy Fleckhaus
Germany

Twen
Issue date: 1962
Art director:
Willy Fleckhaus
Germany

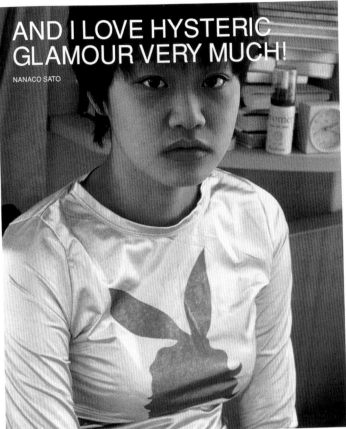

AND I LOVE HYSTERIC GLAMOUR VERY MUCH!

NANACO SATO

Ray Gun
Issue: Aug 1996
Art director:
Robert Hales
USA
Photographer:
Nanaco Sato

Flaunt
Issue:
Fall/Winter 1998
Art directors:
Eric Roinestad,
Jim Turner,
Gerome Vizmanos
USA

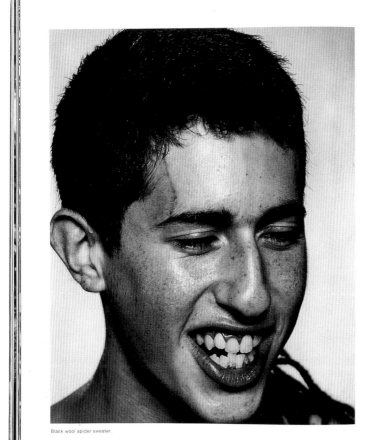

Black wool spider sweater.

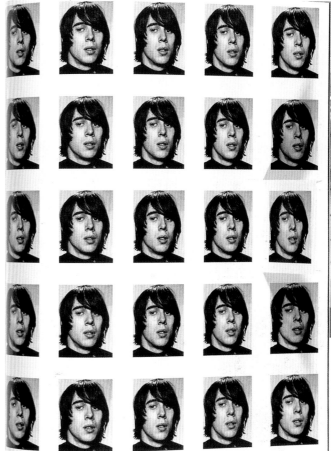

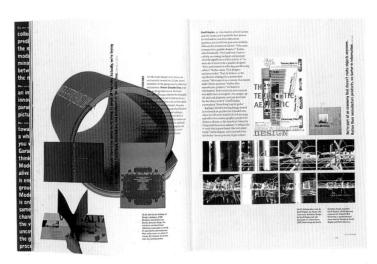

Eye
Issue: 31,
Spring 1999
Art director:
Nick Bell
UK

Blue
Issue: Dec 1998
Art director:
Christa Skinner
and David Carson
Photographer:
Zana Briski
USA

Black + White
Issue: Feb 1999
Art director:
Andrew Godfrey
Photographer:
Kiren Chang
Australia

ALEKSANDRA VUJ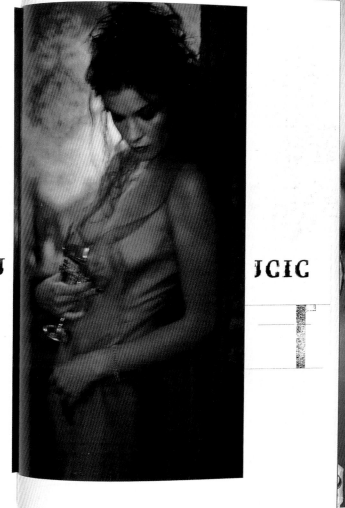JCIC

ALT

FROM WAR-TORN YUGOSLAVIA TO LA VIA NEW ZEALAND, AUSTRALIA AND TWO FEATURE FILMS,
ALEKSANDRA VUJCIC HAS DISCOVERED A PASSION FOR ACTING. OR HAS IT DISCOVERED HER? ➤

In the wider world of graphic design, illustration suffers from periodic peaks and troughs in popularity. But even accounting for the swings of fashion, illustration always has, and continues to be used widely in magazine design.

An art director may choose to use illustration in instances where, for example, the text relates not to a specific place or person, but to a more general mood or theme. While photography relies on the existence of a physical object to photograph, illustrators are only constrained by their imaginations. Magazines dealing with intangibles are heavily reliant on illustration, both technical and abstract, to support features on breakthroughs in thought or scientific discovery, for example; concepts or ideas which may only exist in the mind, or in the darkest recesses of a supercomputer, are brought to life through illustration.

Similarly, fashion magazines are heavily reliant on illustration – a tradition dating back to the days before it was possible to take colour photographs of catwalk shows: today, by accentuating a line, or exaggerating a model's shape an illustrator can convey the sense of a garment, an emotional response to it – rather than its real qualities.

But illustration has other appealing qualities beyond giving visual expression to non-existent entities: words can be incorporated seamlessly into illustration in a way that is impossible in photographs. The aesthetic qualities of hand-rendered images also have their place in magazine design, as they can have a warm, human feel to them which readers find appealing and attractive.

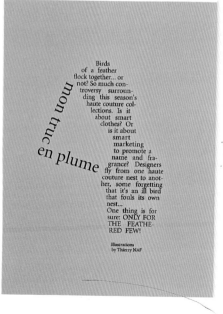

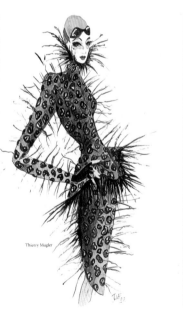

Vogue
Issue: Jul 1995
Art director:
Donald Schneider
Illustrator:
Kim Johnson
France

Vogue
Issue: Jul 1995
Art director:
Donald Schneider
Illustrator:
René Gruan
France

Dutch
Issue: Spring 1997
Art director:
Guido van Lier
Illustrator:
Thierry NAF
Holland

Flaunt
Issue:
Fall/Winter 1998
Art directors:
Eric Roinestad,
Jim Turner,
Gerome Vizmanos
Illustrator:
Malcolm Hill
USA

THE REAL TECHNOLOGY
BEHIND ALL OF OUR OTHER TECHNOLOGIES

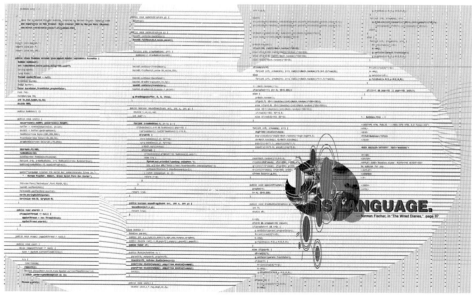

IS LANGUAGE.
—Norman Fischer, in "The Wired Diaries," page 97

THE SELFISH GIANT

The world's richest man is on trial. His multi-billion-dollar software empire, which has dominated the world of personal computers throughout the 1990s, stands accused by the US government of using bully-boy tactics to keep things that way. But if Bill Gates and Microsoft win, they will rule the Internet. Paul Eddy investigates. Illustration: Nick Thornton-Jones

Wired
Issue: Jan 1999
Art director:
Thomas Schneider
USA

The Sunday Times
Magazine
Issue: Mar 1999
Art director:
Andrew McConochie
Illustration:
Nick Thornton Jones
UK

Systems

**Interview
with Vince Frost**

Few editorial designers can boast the diversity of experience accrued by Vince Frost in just the last five years. The London-based art director has worked on a customer magazine, a newspaper supplement, a monthly glossy, an avant-garde style magazine, a newspaper, and an in-house journal. He's worked on foreign language magazines, and art directed publications in three different countries. It's an unlikely mix, and one that gives him a unique perspective on the magazine world.

Frost's introduction to editorial design came when he was working at the design company Pentagram. John Rushworth, a Pentagram partner, had won the contract to produce *P*, a customer magazine for the photographic company Polaroid, and Frost was assigned to help him design it. It proved to be a decisive experience, as much because it opened the designer up to the potential of photography as because it was the first rung on the ladder of editorial design. In fact, the two are intertwined as it was through Frost's newly adopted policy of seeing every photographer who phoned – up to ten a day' that he met and befriended the Douglas brothers, a connection that would later lead to his move from Pentagram to *Big*, a fledgling style magazine produced at that time from Madrid.

P magazine was distributed free of charge to Polaroid's customers across Europe – 'it had a cover price but it was more of a glorified brochure,' remembers Frost. Because it was bankrolled by Polaroid, which wanted it to suggest that it was giving something back to the industry that it served, the magazine had a generous budget, and Frost experimented with expensive finishing effects such as metallic inks and varnishes.

Without the same constraints as a commercial publication, there was time and money to spend on the detailing of *P*. These luxuries were to be in short supply on Frost's next project, and the first of what the designer considers to be his 'signature' magazines – *Big*. It was Frost's friendship with the Douglas brothers, developed during the course of his work on *P*, that netted him a commission to create a series of spreads reserved for guest designers in *Big*. The publisher was so taken with Frost's work that he offered him the job of art director. At *Big*, Frost was left to his own devices as an art director, and even had an unusual level of editorial input. Although the magazine lived up to its name in terms of size, financially it was a small-scale affair. In the absence of a sub-editor, Frost had to devise headlines for content he didn't understand (the magazine was written in Spanish, which he does not speak). The first issue, on New York, set the style. Frost worked with typographer Alan Kitching to create letterpress headlines that were kept short and simple, and styled to visually echo the accompanying photographs. Hence, the spiky, sky-scraper skyline typography of New York. This freedom, born out of the difficult circumstances in which the magazine was produced, is unusual, but proved crucial to the magazine's success, as *Big* came to be characterised by its stunning photography and conceptual typography. 'I have a strong idea, and then do as little as possible to get the idea to work,' is how Frost remembers his approach to *Big*.

Just as Frost's first move was from a generously funded customer magazine with high production values to a small circulation, experimental style magazine, so his next move defied logic: 'The *Independent Magazine* came through doing *Big* magazine,' Frost explains. 'The editor saw *Big* magazine, and I think he just didn't understand what design was about, or what *Big* magazine was, because there was no relationship between them.' Whether or not its editor realised that the conceptual type and tight, uncomfortable grid of a Spanish style magazine were unsuitable for the *Independent* newspaper's weekly colour supplement, Frost certainly understood that the new project called for a radically different approach. The original brief was to design a framework that could be handed over to the paper's in-house designers for week-to-week production. In the event, Frost stayed on as art director for nearly a year. Because of the punishing production schedules of the newspaper world, and the presence of other designers on the team, Frost had neither the luxuries of time and budget available on *P*, nor the wild freedom of *Big*. The result was a reflection of those circumstances: the templates had to take account of the fact that the art director would not always be on hand to supervise production, and the rules had to be obvious to all involved. Frost's design was clean and unfussy, with only one typeface used throughout, creating an elegant, modern look.

02/09/95

Independent
Magazine

Can Britain bite back?

DIVORCE

Big
The nature of *Big*'s young, style-
conscious readers allowed Frost
to experiment with the magazine –
a process which is most obvious
in the contents pages which differ
from issue to issue.

Having set up the templates, Frost's main input was the magazine's covers; he convinced the newspaper's staff that as a supplement, the cover needed neither an enormous masthead nor extensive cover lines, and quickly developed a distinctive style: the cover of each issue took the form of a white space, against which background an icon was positioned, denoting the main story of the week: the Christmas quiz was represented by a question mark composed of seasonal baubles; 'the state of Britain' by a playful bulldog; an article on wives who kill their husbands was marked by a large kitchen knife stuck into the white background, with blood seeping from the 'wound'. For an article on riots in France, he initially considered setting fire to his wife's Citröen 2CV, but fortunately found a replacement model before press day.

Frost's stint as a newspaper supplement designer came to an end when he was recruited to design an edition of the world's most famous glossy magazine: *Vogue*. Publisher Condé Nast wanted to launch a Japanese version of its international fashion magazine, and having seen Frost's work, approached him with the offer of a job. Again, it was a move that seemed to bear no relation to the type of magazine work for which Frost was known: My work has never attracted the same kind of job,' says Frost now. 'After *Big*, the *Independent* came along. And then *Vogue* – where the hell did *Vogue* come from?' In the end, 'creative differences' led Frost to retire from the project after three months, but his time at Japanese *Vogue* neatly completed a circle, begun when he had indulged his 'fascination with the glossiness and slickness of women's magazines' while designing *P* magazine.

Frost's next step is to become his own client, designing and producing a magazine about 'whatever's interesting at the time'. Having worked on magazines published by a newspaper, a charity (D&AD), a big corporation, a tiny independent publisher and the multi-billion dollar Condé Nast, Frost feels he has the measure of magazines: 'There's no mystery behind the stuff we do for other people,' he says. 'It's just having an idea.' Perhaps it's the only logical step for a designer whose illogical steps mean he's done everything else.

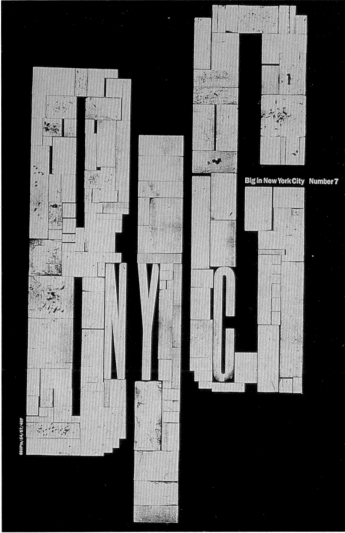

Big in New York City   Number 7

Although every magazine feature is made attractive and navigable by design, the designer's craft is particularly important where the feature is not a narrative made up by words, pictures or both, but a set of figures or series of pieces of information that assume their significance from the way that they are juxtaposed with one another. Examples include maps, charts, timelines, tables, comparisons and lists (50 ways to leave your lover; what's hot, and what's not). On those occasions, one could almost say that design, or the way the page is laid out, becomes the story.

Permutations of all the devices listed above make regular appearances in magazines. Some are just a comparatively easy way for uninspired writers to fill a page. Others, however, allow the communication of a lot of complex information in a way that is both easy to interpret and interesting to read, in a comparatively small space. The designer requires not only a sensitive approach to the handling of type and image, but also a thorough and intelligent grasp of the subject in hand, in order to devise an appropriate information system.

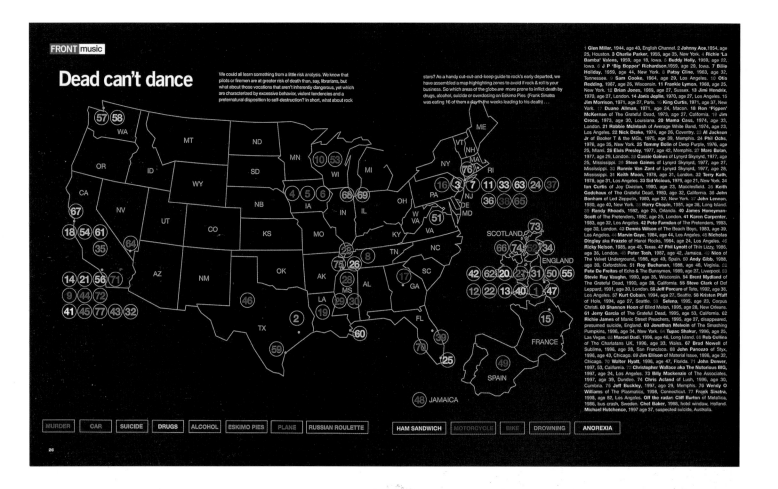

Gear
Issue: Jan/Feb 1999
Art director:
Matthew Guemple
USA

Van
Issue: Oct 1998
Art director:
Fernando Gutiérrez
Spain

Van
Issue: Oct 1998
Art director:
Fernando Gutiérrez
Spain

NUEVA YORK

La ciudad más cosmopolita de los Estados Unidos prepara la llegada de su semana de la moda. La estrellas de Hollywood pisan el asfalto de la gran manzana para asistir a los desfiles de Calvin Klein o Donna Karan pero cuando los shows toquen a su fin, el trepidante ritmo de la ciudad no les echará de menos.

1. Hotel Mercer. 99. Prince Street. T .9666060. El hotel con más encanto (donde se alojan todas las modelos y los mejores críticos de moda).

2. Las carpas de la calle 42 han sido tradicionalmente el lugar donde se han celebrado todos los desfiles de la Semana de la Moda neoyorkina. Este año habrá sorpresas para la parroquia del Fashion System, que sufrirá los rigores del tráfico de la ciudad de los rascacielos (y sus atascos) para asistir a los shows.

3. Asia de Cuba. Morgans Hotel. 237 Madison Avenue. Uno de los mejores restaurantes de la ciudad, especializado en comida chino-latina y diseñado por el genial Philippe Starck.

4. Balthazar. 80 Spring Street. Restaurante del Soho donde encontrarás famosos, muchas, muchas modelos y un rebuscado ambiente de brasserie parisina.

5. Life/The Ki Club. 158 Bleeckler Street. El club del modelo por excelencia. A él asiste todo aquel que quiere dejarse ver.

6. Lift-Off. 104 Prince Street. Los zapatos más alucinantes de John Fluevog, una especie de versión urbana de los que lleva Celia Cruz.

7. Pop Shop. 292 Lafayette. La tienda donde encontrar todo tipo de cosas al estilo Keith Haring. Los beneficios son para su fundación contra el SIDA.

8. Route 146. 146 Sullivan Street. Accesorios hechos con materia prima barata: basura reciclada. Son más que increíbles.

FW

ESTRUCTURA VISUAL   FICHATÉCNICA

PUNTOS DE VENTA donde encontrarás las prendas y complementos de nuestros editoriales de moda ordenados visualmente para su mejor localización. Este mes el gris, los jeans y la lycía han sido los grandes protagonistas.

PERFECT SHAPES (estilista) DAH-LEN

GIANFRANCO FERRE para más información: T. 915440233. HUGO BOSS Avda. Diagonal, 574, Barcelona. T. 93-2033222. Para más información: T. 913635333. COSTUME NATIONAL. De día a Castop, Villanueva, 3. Madrid T. 915777728. JEAN PAUL GAULTIER Exception. Velázquez, 28. Madrid T. 915774964. TRUSSARDI 41 Jean Pier Bus. Avda Diagonal, 463. Barc. T. 934597120. ALEXANDER MC QUEEN Beautiful People. Size, 20. Madrid, T. 914316769. MOSCHINO T. 91.9940233. DOLCE & GABBANA Exception. Velázquez, 28. Madrid, T. 915774964. GIORGIO ARMANI Ortega y Gasset, 21. Madrid. T. 914351308. EXEXPTION Velázquez, 28. Madrid, T. 915774964. ICEBERG Exception. Velázquez, 28. T. 915774964. HELMUT LANG Pza. 2. Armario, 22. T. 915223311.

WILD JEANS (estilista) GUY ARDUCH

RALPH BY RALPH LAURENTE: Cortes Inglés. PATRICK COX. Beautiful People. Goya, 20. T. 914316769. GUESS T. 934195429. HELMUT LANG Pza. 2. Armario, 22. T. 915223311. MOSCHINO JEANS T. 91 9940233. FUTURE OZBEK. Beautiful People. Goya, 20. T. 914316769. CK BY CALVIN KLEIN El Corte Inglés. (próxima apertura de tienda en Madrid). DIESEL T. 935181623. D&S para más información: T. 915440233. PAT FIELD MY Boqán. T. 915223121. EMPORIO ARMANI Claudio Coello, 32. T. 914351305. JOOP Sprüng e Castillo. Villanueva, 3. T. 915777729.

PRIVATE SHOTS (estilista) GIORGIO GATTI

TRUSSARDI Jean Pierre Bus. Avda Diagonal, 463. T. 93439710. ICEBERG Exception. Velázquez, 28. T. 915774964. MOSCHINO LINGERIE T. 919940233. D&S T. 915440233. ALESSANDRO DELL'ACQUA para más información: T. 915446286. CALLADWAR Exception. Velázquez, 28. T. 915774964. LEVI'S Sardis Levi's en toda España. CONVERSE en las mejores tiendas del ramo. AMAYA ARZUAGA Burgos T. 947171717. PARIS T. 915446706665. Loewe. T. 44171344123. GUCCI Don Ramón de la Cruz, 2. T. 914311717. SERGIO ROSSI Exception. Velázquez, 28. T. 915774964.

116 Y 16.98

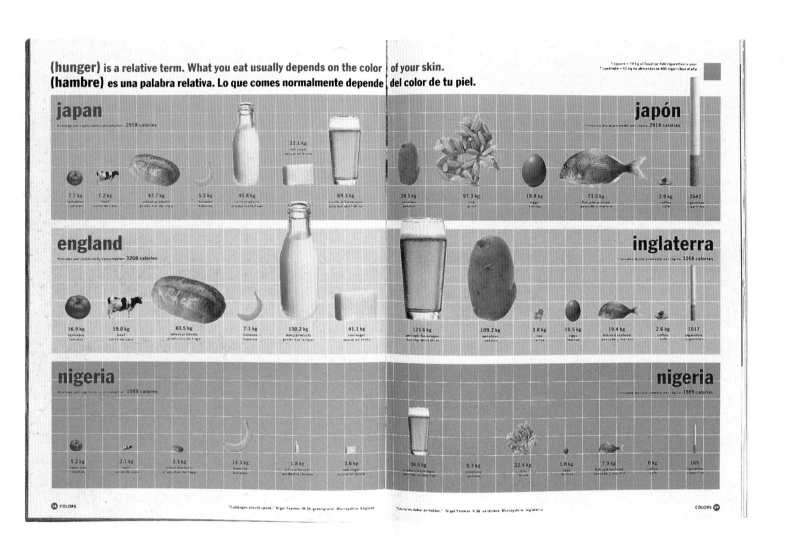

(hunger) is a relative term. What you eat usually depends on the color | of your skin.
(hambre) es una palabra relativa. Lo que comes normalmente depende | del color de tu piel.

¹ square = 10 kg of food (or 400 cigarettes) a year
¹ cuadrado = 10 kg de alimentos (o 400 cigarrillos) al año

japan
Average per capita daily consumption: 2918 calories

| 7.7 kg tomatoes tomates | 7.2 kg beef carne de vaca | 43.7 kg wheat products productos de trigo | 5.2 kg bananas bananas | 45.8 kg dairy products productos lácteos | 69.3 kg alcoholic beverages bebidas alcohólicas | 22.1 kg raw sugar azúcar en bruto |

japón
Consumo diario promedio per cápita: 2918 calorías

| 28.5 kg potatoes patatas | 97.3 kg rice arroz | 18.8 kg eggs huevos | 73.5 kg fish and seafood pescado y marisco | 2.9 kg coffee café | 2642 cigarettes cigarrillos |

england
Average per capita daily consumption: 3268 calories

| 16.9 kg tomatoes tomates | 19.0 kg beef carne de vaca | 83.5 kg wheat products productos de trigo | 7.1 kg bananas bananas | 130.2 kg dairy products productos lácteos | 41.1 kg raw sugar azúcar en bruto |

inglaterra
Consumo diario promedio per cápita: 3268 calorías

| 123.6 kg alcoholic beverages bebidas alcohólicas | 109.2 kg potatoes patatas | 3.8 kg rice arroz | 10.5 kg eggs huevos | 19.4 kg fish and seafood pescado y marisco | 2.6 kg coffee café | 1017 cigarettes cigarrillos |

nigeria
Average per capita daily consumption: 1989 calories

| 5.2 kg tomatoes tomates | 2.1 kg beef carne de vaca | 2.3 kg wheat products productos de trigo | 14.3 kg bananas bananas | 1.8 kg dairy products productos lácteos | 3.6 kg raw sugar azúcar en bruto |

nigeria
Consumo diario promedio per cápita: 1989 calorías

| 36.0 kg alcoholic beverages bebidas alcohólicas | 0.3 kg potatoes patatas | 22.4 kg rice arroz | 1.8 kg eggs huevos | 7.9 kg fish and seafood pescado y marisco | 0 kg coffee café | 165 cigarettes cigarrillos |

"Cabbages should speak." Nigel Yeoman, M 36 greengrocer. Murrayshire, England
"Las coles deberían hablar." Nigel Yeoman, V 36 verdulero, Murrayshire, Inglaterra

Colors
Issue: 6
Editor-in-chief:
Tibor Kalman
Design: Scott Stowell
Italy

Colors
Issue: 25
Creative editor:
Adam Broomberg
Designer:
Runyon Hall
Italy

Neue Graphik
Issue: 17/18/1965
Art directors:
Richard P. Lohse
J. Müller-Brockmann
Hans Neuberg
Carlo L. Vivarelli
Switzerland

How fat
is your
world?

Quant'è
grasso il tuo
mondo?

Per mantenerci sani
dovremmo consumare
2.600 calorie al giorno (l'equivalente di cinque Big Mac).
I paesi più ricchi (Giappone, Stati Uniti, Francia)
banchettano con il 140% di questo quantitativo,
il doppio rispetto ai paesi più poveri (Sudan, Madagascar, Laos).
In questa cartina abbiamo modellato gli stati più grassi o più magri,
a seconda di quanto mangiano.
Credi che il tuo paese
abbia bisogno di mettersi a dieta?

To stay healthy,
we should all consume
2,600 calories a day. (About five Big Macs.)
The richest countries in the world (Japan, USA, France)
feast on 140 percent of this, twice as many
calories as the poorest (Sudan, Madagascar, Laos).
On this map, we've made countries fatter or thinner
according to how much they eat.
Does your homeland
need to diet?

80 COLORS

COLORS 81

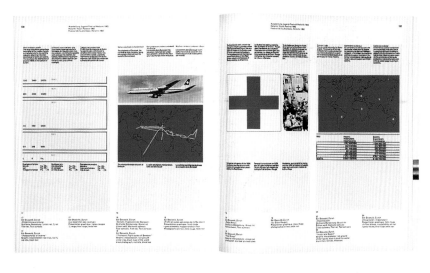

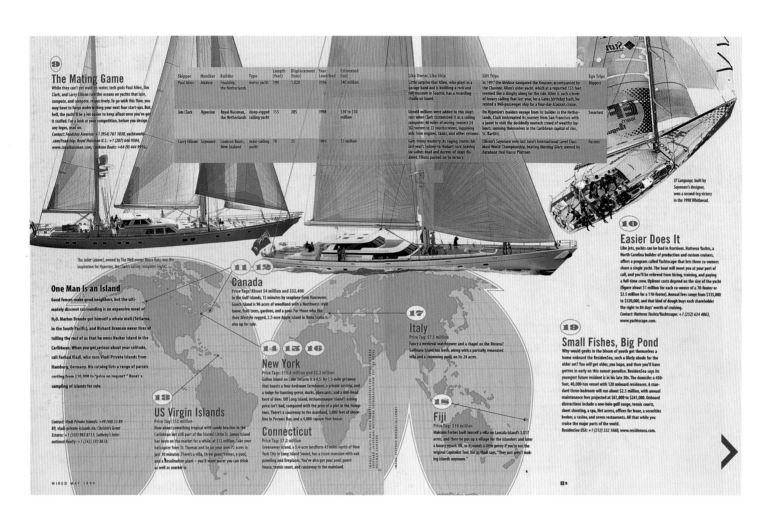

⑨ The Mating Game

While they can't yet walk on water, tech gods Paul Allen, Jim Clark, and Larry Ellison rule the oceans on yachts that laze, compute, and compete, respectively. To go with this flow, you may have to forgo underwriting your next four start-ups. But, hell, the yacht'll be a lot easier to keep afloat once you've got it staffed. For a look at your competition, before you design any logos, read on.

Contact: Feadship America: +1 (954) 761 1830, yachtworld.com/feadship; Royal Huisman U.S.: +1 (207) 646 9504, www.royalhuisman.com; Cookson Boats: +64 (9) 444 9915.

Skipper	Moniker	Builder	Type	Length (feet)	Displacement (tons)	Year Launched	Estimated Cost	Like Owner, Like Ship	Gilt Trips	Ego Trips
Paul Allen	*Médése*	Feadship, the Netherlands	motor yacht	199	1,028	1996	$40 million	Little surprise that Allen, who plays in a garage band and is building a rock and roll museum in Seattle, has a recording studio on board.	In 1997 the *Médése* navigated the Amazon, accompanied by the *Charade*, Allen's older yacht, which at a reported 153 feet seemed like a dinghy along for the ride. Allen is such a lover of luxury sailing that last year, for a Gates birthday bash, he rented a 960-passenger ship for a four-day Alaskan cruise.	Biggest
Jim Clark	*Hyperion*	Royal Huisman, the Netherlands	sloop-rigged sailing yacht	155	285	1998	$30 to $50 million	Untold millions were added to this ship's cost when Clark customized it as a sailing computer; 40 miles of wiring connect 24 SGI servers to 22 touchscreens, supplying info from engines, tanks, and other systems.	On *Hyperion*'s maiden voyage from its builder in the Netherlands, Clark interrupted its journey from San Francisco with a jaunt to visit the decidedly nontech crowd of wealthy layabouts sunning themselves in the Caribbean capital of chic, St. Barth's.	Smartest
Larry Ellison	*Sayonara*	Cookson Boats, New Zealand	maxi-sailing yacht	78	25	1995	$3 million	Guts trump modesty. As raging storms hit last year's Sydney-to-Hobart race, leaving six sailors dead and dozens of ships disabled, Ellison pushed on to victory.	Ellison's *Sayonara* won June's International Level Class Maxi World Championship, beating *Morning Glory*, owned by database rival Hasso Plattner.	Fastest

EF Language, built by *Sayonara*'s designer, won a second-leg victory in the 1998 Whitbread.

The *Juliet* (above), owned by The Well owner Bruce Katz, was the inspiration for *Hyperion*, Jim Clark's sailing computer (right).

One Man Is an Island

Good fences make good neighbors, but the ultimately discreet surrounding is an expansive moat of H₂O. Marlon Brando got himself a whole atoll (Tetiaroa, in the South Pacific), and Richard Branson never tires of telling the rest of us that he owns Necker Island in the Caribbean. When you get serious about your solitude, call Farhad Vladi, who runs Vladi Private Islands from Hamburg, Germany. His catalog lists a range of parcels costing from $70,000 to "price on request." Here's a sampling of islands for sale.

Contact: Vladi Private Islands: +49 (40) 33 89 89, vladi-private-islands.de; Christie's Great Estates: +1 (505) 983 8733; Sotheby's International Realty: +1 (242) 393 8618.

⑪ ⑫ Canada
Price Tags: About $4 million and $32,400
In the Gulf Islands, 15 minutes by seaplane from Vancouver, Gooch Island is 96 acres of woodland with a Northwest-style home, fruit trees, gardens, and a pool. For those who like their lifestyle rugged, 2.5-acre Apple Island in Nova Scotia is also up for sale.

⑬ US Virgin Islands
Price Tag: $12 million
How about something tropical with sandy beaches in the Caribbean but still part of the States? Little St. James Island has been on the market for a while, at $12 million. Take your helicopter from St. Thomas and be on your own 72 acres in just 10 minutes. There's a villa, three guest homes, a pool, and a desalination plant – you'll want water you can drink as well as snorkel in.

⑭ ⑮ ⑯ New York
Price Tags: $10.4 million and $2.3 million
Galloo Island on Lake Ontario is a 4.5- by 1.5-mile getaway that boasts a four-bedroom farmhouse, a private airstrip, and a lodge for hunting geese, ducks, pheasants, and a 600-head herd of deer. Off Long Island, Arshamonoque Island's asking price isn't bad, compared with the price of a plot in the Hamptons. There's a causeway to the mainland, 3,000 feet of shoreline in Peconic Bay, and a 4,800-square foot house.

Connecticut
Price Tag: $7.2 million
Greenaway Island, a 3.4-acre landform 43 miles north of New York City in Long Island Sound, has a stone mansion with oak paneling and fireplaces. You've also got your pool, guest house, tennis court, and causeway to the mainland.

⑰ Italy
Price Tag: $7.5 million
Fancy a medieval watchtower and a chapel on the Riviera? Gallinara Island has both, along with a partially renovated villa and a swimming pool, on its 24 acres.

⑱ Fiji
Price Tag: $10 million
Malcolm Forbes built himself a villa on Laucala Island's 3,017 acres, and then he put up a village for the islanders and later a luxury resort. OK, so it sounds a little pricey if you're not the original Capitalist Tool, but as Vladi says, "They just aren't making islands anymore."

⑩ Easier Does It

Like jets, yachts can be had in fractions. Hatteras Yachts, a North Carolina builder of production and custom cruisers, offers a program called Yachtscape that lets three co-owners share a single yacht. The boat will meet you at your port of call, and you'll be relieved from hiring, training, and paying a full-time crew. Upfront costs depend on the size of the yacht (figure about $1 million for each co-owner of a 70-footer or $2.5 million for a 110-footer). Annual fees range from $135,000 to $320,000, and that kind of dough buys each shareholder the right to 84 days' worth of cruising.

Contact: Hatteras Yachts/Yachtscape: +1 (252) 634 4863, www.yachtscape.com.

⑲ Small Fishes, Big Pond

Why would geeks in the bloom of youth get themselves a home onboard the ResidenSea, such a likely abode for the older set? You will get older, you hope, and then you'll have gotten in early on this sunset paradise. ResidenSea says its youngest future resident is in his late 30s. The domicile: a 450-foot, 40,000-ton vessel with 120 onboard residences. A standard three-bedroom will run about $2.5 million, with annual maintenance fees projected at $61,000 to $241,000. Onboard distractions include a one-hole golf range, tennis courts, skeet shooting, a spa, Net access, offices for lease, a securities broker, a casino, and seven restaurants. All that while you cruise the major ports of the world.

ResidenSea USA: +1 (212) 332 1660, www.residensea.com.

WIRED MAY 1999

89

Wired
Issue: May 1999
Art director:
Thomas Schneider
USA

Wired
Issue: May 1999
Art director:
Thomas Schneider
USA

Creative Review
Issue: May 1999
Art director:
Nathan Gale
UK

Frieze
Issue: Apr 1999
Art director:
Tom Gidley
UK

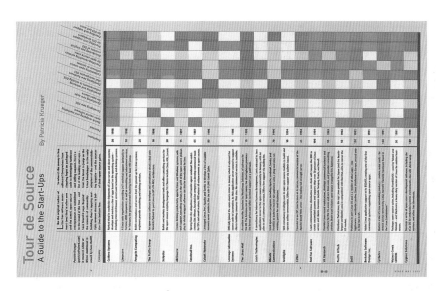

Webzines

Interview
with Roger Black
Similarities and differences
Dual versions
The future

**Interview
with Roger Black**

Like Paul Rand before him, Roger Black had an early start as an art director, cutting his teeth on a short-lived tabloid magazine, *LA*, aged 23. Since then his work on titles such as *Rolling Stone* (1975–78), *Newsweek* (1985–86) and *Esquire* (1991 and 1993) have brought him to the attention of publishers the world over, and he has designed or redesigned literally hundreds of magazines in his homeland, the US, and abroad: publications in Switzerland, Italy, Spain, France, Germany, Mexico, Brazil and Canada have all received the Black treatment.

In recent years, however, Black has arguably become as well known for his work in a new medium as he is for his editorial design in print. In 1994 he took the plunge and entered the relatively new world of design for the World Wide Web. The company he founded in 1994, the Interactive Bureau, now has offices on both the East and West Coasts of the United States.

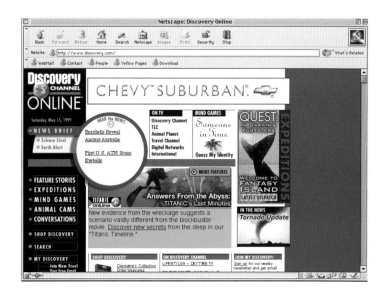

Despite his full immersion in new media, however, Black has not entirely turned his back on print, and magazines in particular. Indeed, Black is of the opinion that the two are inextricably linked, as it is impossible for a designer to work effectively in print today without an understanding of new media: 'The typical feeling is that you can only do one thing at a time. In this era you have to do both,' he insists. Black suggests that working in print without having an understanding of the web is analogous to designing magazines in the 1970s without understanding television – you don't have to be directing shows but you must understand other forms of media in order to attune your own particular strand to the more general needs and concerns of users. Indeed, in Black's view, the growth of new media co-incides with another shift in the design business: 'There are a number of design areas that have been practiced in isolation,' he explains. 'Corporate literature is produced separately from corporate identity, publications or design for advertising. Now we're understanding that people have to be moving in the same direction, and maybe even working on the same team.'

But where does the designer of print magazines fit into this new model? According to Black, editorial design is the ideal background for a prospective web designer, whether the client is an on-line magazine or a corporate megalith. Today, on-line magazines make up only a small fraction of the Interactive Bureau's on-line work. So what does this collection of former magazine designers have to offer the major corporate client looking for a web site? 'The skills that magazine designers have are incredibly useful in the world outside magazines,' insists Black. How? Well first, magazine designers are unwitting brand experts, who have been producing some of the strongest brands around for years – most owners of consumer product brands would kill for the recognition factor of *Vogue*, or the extent to which those hard-to-reach consumers, the younger readers of men's magazines such as *Maxim* or *Playboy*, identify with their brand. As Black puts it: 'One of the things that magazine designers do well, that they don't realise they do, is defining the brand way beyond the design of a logotype. Most magazine brands are vastly more expressive than consumer brands have ever been.'

Furthermore, the web is an essentially open medium – access for all and freedom of information are its *raison d'être*. Much has been made of the fact that through e-commerce or on-line auctions, items can be bought, sold or exchanged on the web. But what is often overlooked is that most of the swaps taking place are of information, and 'the fact is that information transactions are a magazine idea. The corporate design world, which once existed to protect the CEO and the board from the public, is now taking a very magazine-like approach to the public.'

The conventional wisdom of brands is that they should be the same every time you come across them: If you buy a McDonald's in Times Square, it will have the same packaging as one bought in Red Square. There are two exceptions to this rule: magazines, where readers want them to be identifiably the same, but appreciably different every issue, and the web, where because of the nature of the medium, users want to find new information, new features, new ideas each time they log on to a site. Magazine designers have learned how to do this.

Black also suggests that more websites, whether they are on-line magazines or 'brochureware' (on-line promotional literature) could benefit from some of the design rules employed by magazines: 'Components of magazine design are exactly what most websites need,' he argues. 'More visual information; a hierarchy of text – sub-heads, decks and pull quotes. After all, the download time for text is virtually zero – so why can't we have some picture captions?' In his 1997 book, *Web Sites That Work*, Black argued that ten rules that 'have underpinned good print design for hundreds of years are equally valid on-line'. The rules for print are: put content on every page; the first colour is white; the second colour is black; the third colour is red; never letterspace lower case; never set a lot of type in all caps; a cover should be a poster; use only one or two typefaces; make everything as big as possible; and get lumpy – surprise the reader with varying distributions of content throughout the magazine. For the web, however, he added ten more: don't

repurpose (don't redesign bits of the magazine for the web unless they work better that way); don't confuse the reader – stay consistent, make sure navigational devices are simple and clear; don't make oversize pages – be aware of users with smaller monitors; don't design pages that require scrolling – people won't read them; don't use big slow graphics; don't use a lot of colours – it looks bad; don't use blurry drop shadows – they look worse; don't have a lot of text – users won't read it; and don't use tiny type – reading from a screen is harder than reading from a page.

Has anything changed since Black wrote the book? 'The main change, that was beginning to happen in 1997, is that the utility uses of the Net would massively outnumber the editorial uses.' In other words, the Net would be used not for reading at great length, but rather for those instant information 'transactions' referred to earlier. Users go on-line looking for one specific piece of information – how the weather will change over the next hour, or who won the 1947 World Series – and sites must meet those requirements. This is in part the job of the editor and the technician, who might optimise the site for the sort of algorithmic searches performed by search engines. But design also has a role to play: text should be presented in easily manageable chunks; a reader waiting for the answer to a specific enquiry – the current price of a particular stock, for example – should not have to wait for a complex page to be updated in its entirety.

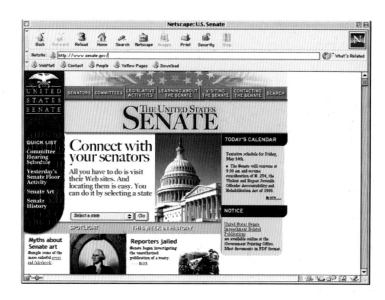

Black is also keen to stress that publishing on the web does differ from design for print in at least one area of critical importance: in *Web Sites That Work* he described it as 'the move from a one-way paradigm to a two-way paradigm'. On the web, the user always has a degree of input into the way they view the site: unlike conventional publishing, where every reader is obliged to read the magazine in the same format as it left the printer, web designers must be aware that inconsistencies between the hardware set-up of different readers will mean that the site must be flexible, and the the designer cannot afford to be too precious about variations within an overall framework.

Aside from technical constraints over which they have no control, the reader may wish to exercise direct control over the content of a site, whether it be personalising it, in the case of fast-growing 'portal' sites such as Yahoo and Excite, or by adding their own contributions in the form of chat or deposits on message boards – on-line newsgroups were the forerunner of the web after all. Even where sites have such facilities, however, designers have generally been slow to realise that they should be a central feature of on-line publishing. As Black puts it: 'What hasn't happened, that I expected to happen, is a greater use of the communications function of the Net. You don't see chat folded into websites in a very integral way – pull quotes from live chats updated to the home page for example.' Black attributes this to the fact that there are currently very few sites that are updated constantly in real time – they are operated on the book publishing model, rather than the TV model, which in many respects they are closer to.

These are general criticisms and observations, based on what Black brings as an experienced magazine designer to the subject of web design as a whole. But what of on-line magazines in particular? As far as print-to-web transfers go, Black suggests that the magazine, by its compendious, eclectic nature, is well suited to make the transition, but he is constantly surprised by the extent to which the designers of on-line magazines neglect or reject the equities built up so painstakingly in the print versions: either they change their names, or misuse the logo, or attempt to add a sense of technological glamour by dispensing with a perfectly functional aspect of the print design for the on-line version.

A potential difficulty experienced by the print designer moving into design for the web is in the area of navigation: in *Web Sites That Work*, Black is insistent about the importance of clear navigation and a logical site architecture. But he plays down the extent to which the print designer might find themselves in unfamiliar territory once on-line: 'I think that a good designer doesn't have to stretch very far. Magazines are usually regarded as being linear but actually they are not: some people start from the middle and read on; some people read backwards. You could just flick to a page and read it forever. A good designer understands that and works for all of those possible behaviours. On the web the number of ways you can navigate a site is amplified by the existence of hypertext links, but the web by its nature is a more flexible and forgiving medium.' Magazine designers, argues Black, are well-used to second guessing readers' habits: 'Which is yet another reason why good magazine designers should do well on the web,' he concludes.

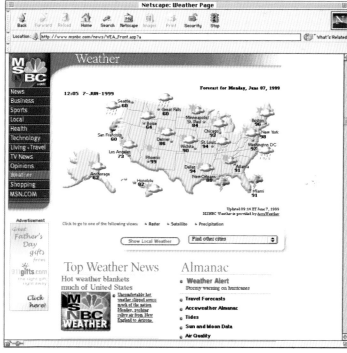

When the editorial designer Roger Black began to design websites, including on-line magazines, in the mid-1990s, he aroused the ire of many of the web's existing users; those who fellow web convert David Siegal described as the 'HTML police' argued that this new medium should evolve in the way that its pioneers wanted, free from the burden of design-historical baggage represented by Black, Siegal and their ilk. Certainly many of the pioneer on-line magazines rejected many of the conventions of print publishing, establishing a new aesthetic and a new way of handling editorial matter.

Today it might be argued that there are two sorts of magazine on the web; the on-line versions of publications that already exist in a print format – from *Cosmopolitan* to *The Economist* – and those that exist solely in cyberspace. Designers of magazines in the former group are effectively constrained by tradition and precedent; they are obliged to create sites that accord with certain of the conventions of their print cousins. The latter group is arguably freer to pursue the construction of an entirely new media. But while it is true that the web is a unique medium, presenting problems that cannot be tackled in the same way as either print magazines or television, it is also demonstrably true that many of the lessons learnt in design for print can, and should, make the transition to the digital interface. Hundreds of years of newspaper, magazine and book publishing have taught designers valuable lessons about what and how people read; from the minor details – where the eye naturally alights on the page – to how much conflicting information the reader can comfortably

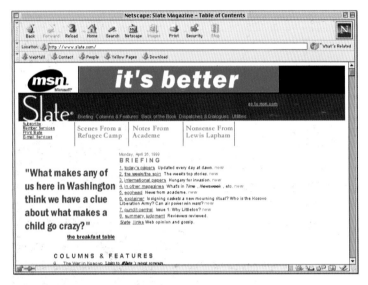

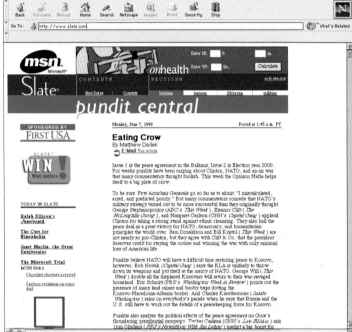

manage at any one time. Those findings are ignored at the on-line publisher's peril. Whether the webzine is a cousin to a print version, or an entirely original venture, the design solution will, inevitably, involve reconciling the requirements of magazines in any format with the demands of the medium.

That said, however, there are real differences between print- and web-based magazines and the transition to the web for the print designer is potentially as challenging as a first time effort for a novice to either medium – unlearning what you do know is often as difficult as learning what you don't. The web presents several advantages over print for the aspiring magazine designer: it is comparatively cheap to produce a magazine on-line, as the publisher does not incur the same production and distribution costs as a print magazine; similarly, an on-line magazine does not compete so directly for readers as it does not have to jostle for prime position on the news-stand with established rivals: once published, it enjoys the same prominence, or lack of it, as any other site. Consequently covers, for example, decline in importance. The medium allows on-line magazine designers to incorporate personalised features, moving images, and sound. Once a reader's attention has been attracted, they can be invited to participate in a dialogue co-ordinated by the magazine, or directed to an archive of material on similar topics. Microsoft's on-line magazine *Slate* (www.slate.com), for example, does both of these things.

The disadvantages inherent in on-line publishing may also come as something of a shock to the designer for print: with current bandwidth limitations, varying monitor sizes and comparatively poor on-screen reproduction quality, certain restrictions are imposed. Readers may be disinclined to wait patiently for large graphics to download, and may even be unwilling to spend long periods reading from a screen. Although, as Bill Gates would have it, information is transmitted across the Net 'at the speed of thought', most users must wait rather longer for it to appear on their screens. While the print magazine designer knows that the reader can just flick past pages that do not interest them, the webzine designer may have a harder time ensuring that the reader's attention and interest are maintained across the whole magazine, despite the irritations of download times.

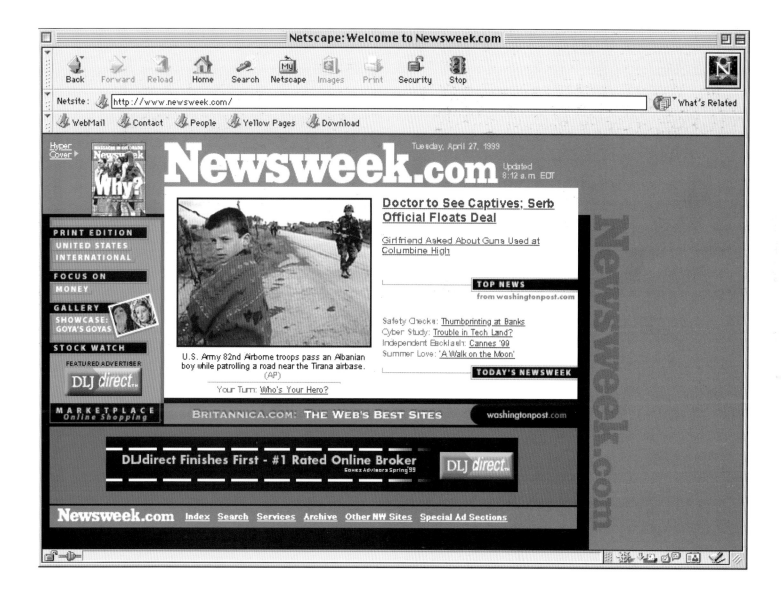

Similarly, readers of print magazines can easily tell whereabouts they are in the magazine; the most obvious way in which this is done is by feel – if you have more pages in your right hand, you're more than halfway through. To return to the contents page at the beginning of the magazine, you simply transfer the rest of the pages from your left hand to your right. This may sound elementary, but it's second nature to readers, and contributes to their sense of familiarity and ease with print publications. Similarly, while print magazines are a self-contained unit, the boundaries of an on-line magazine are less clearly defined: links and click-through advertising, essential components of almost every site, mean that a reader can slip, almost unawares, out of a site. Readers' frustrations with webzines usually arise from getting 'lost', and the architecture and navigability of sites are of critical importance.

Most of these downsides are minor obstacles, however, and are easily overcome: blocks of flat colour are quicker to download, and typefaces adapted specifically for on-line use make for easier reading. Many webzines use devices such as navigation bars or contents tables at the foot of every page to counter the twin problems of orientation (knowing where you are in the bigger picture) and easy movement from page to page. But these are solutions specific to the medium, and involve the designer being prepared and able to ignore some of the rules of print magazine design.

Standards of design across the web are generally fairly low – as one would expect; it began life as a means to exchange academic information and is not a beauty contest. Despite the exponential growth of the web design industry, the vast majority of sites are still designed by individuals with no design training. But as ever greater numbers of readers read webzines instead of, rather than as well as print magazines, the unique advantages of the medium will not compensate for poor readability, uninspiring layouts and a lack of the visually manifested personality with which many print magazines are so redolent.

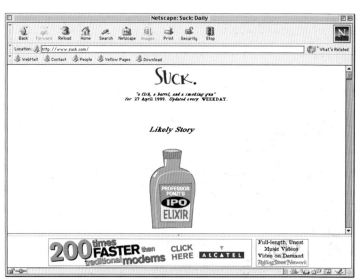

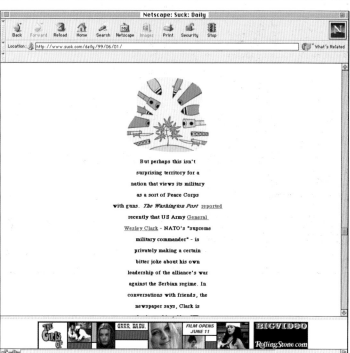

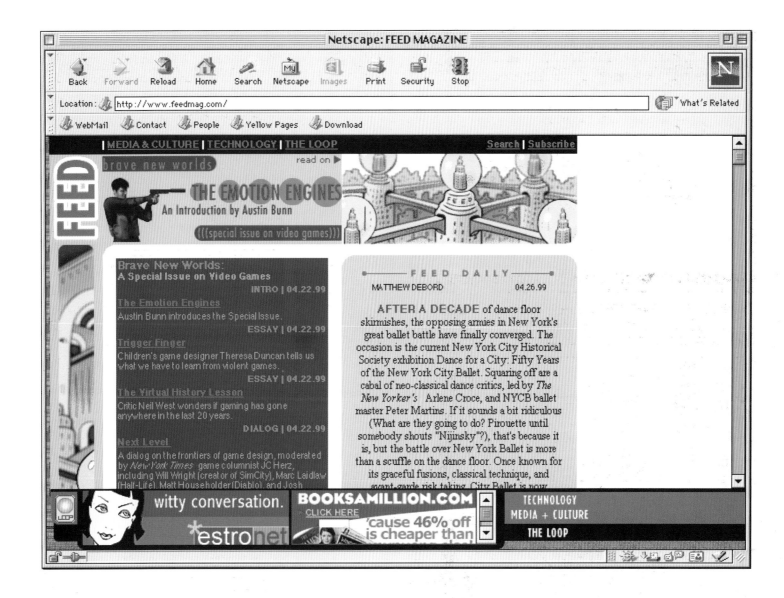

Netscape: FEED MAGAZINE

Back Forward Reload Home Search Netscape Images Print Security Stop

Location : http://www.feedmag.com/   What's Related

WebMail   Contact   People   Yellow Pages   Download

MEDIA & CULTURE | TECHNOLOGY | THE LOOP   Search | Subscribe

brave new worlds   read on ▶

THE EMOTION ENGINES
An Introduction by Austin Bunn

(((special issue on video games)))

Brave New Worlds:
A Special Issue on Video Games
                    INTRO | 04.22.99
The Emotion Engines
Austin Bunn introduces the Special Issue.
                    ESSAY | 04.22.99
Trigger Finger
Children's game designer Theresa Duncan tells us
what we have to learn from violent games.
                    ESSAY | 04.22.99
The Virtual History Lesson
Critic Neil West wonders if gaming has gone
anywhere in the last 20 years.
                    DIALOG | 04.22.99
Next Level
A dialog on the frontiers of game design, moderated
by New York Times game columnist JC Herz,
including Will Wright (creator of SimCity), Marc Laidlaw
(Half-Life), Matt Householder (Diablo), and Josh

FEED DAILY
MATTHEW DEBORD   04.26.99

AFTER A DECADE of dance floor
skirmishes, the opposing armies in New York's
great ballet battle have finally converged. The
occasion is the current New York City Historical
Society exhibition Dance for a City: Fifty Years
of the New York City Ballet. Squaring off are a
cabal of neo-classical dance critics, led by The
New Yorker's Arlene Croce, and NYCB ballet
master Peter Martins. If it sounds a bit ridiculous
(What are they going to do? Pirouette until
somebody shouts "Nijinsky"?), that's because it
is, but the battle over New York Ballet is more
than a scuffle on the dance floor. Once known for
its graceful fusions, classical technique, and
avant-garde risk taking, City Ballet is now

witty conversation.   BOOKSAMILLION.COM   TECHNOLOGY
                              CLICK HERE   MEDIA + CULTURE
astronet   'cause 46% off   THE LOOP
                      is cheaper than

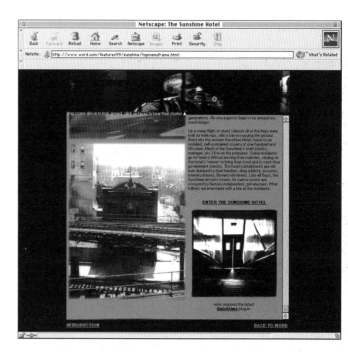

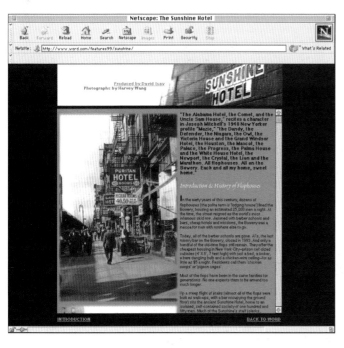

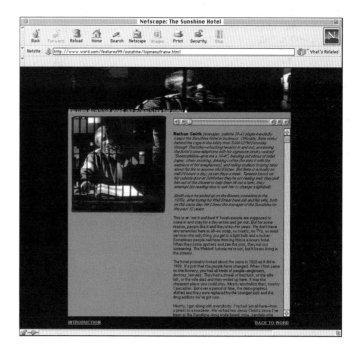

Wired
www.hotwired.com

Word
www.word.com

Cosmopolitan
www.cosmomag.com

In recent years, many publishers of print magazines have realised that however apparently secure their positions, they cannot afford to ignore the new media, and have added a digital element to their offer. In most cases, this is just a website carrying the bare bones of one or two back issues and subscription details. A few of the more forward-looking magazines, however, have used the opportunities provided by digital media to produce a genuinely different version of the magazine on-line or on a CD-ROM.

The on-line version of *Colors* was designed by students at Fabrica, the art school run by Benetton and sited next door to the offices of *Colors* itself. While the content of the two versions is fundamentally the same, and is developed and researched by the staff of *Colors*, the difference is seen in the way that it is handled by the website's designers.

From its inception the Benetton customer magazine has tried to use images as a kind of international language, using photography to tell stories in the way that other magazines would use text. The opportunities offered by the digital media to distort, animate or otherwise enhance the communicative power of these illustrations and diagrams were embraced with alacrity by the designers.

The print version of issue 22, whose theme was 'Hair', contains a feature on the messages conveyed by the hair of newsreaders in different countries. In the on-line version, the content remains the same, but users are able to 'fast-forward' or 'rewind' through the images and accompanying quotes through the use of the familiar directional icons from stereo and VCR sets. Similarly, the print version of issue 25, 'Fat', contains a map made out of coloured dough, entitled 'how fat is

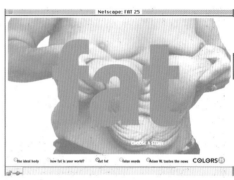

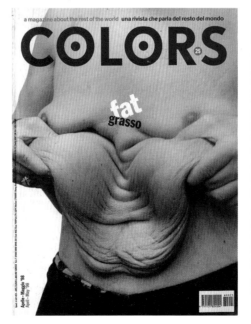

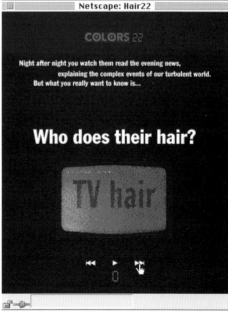

your world?'. The richer countries are represented on the map according to how much of the world's food supply they consume in relation to other, poorer countries. Hence, North America and Europe appear on this map to be many times larger than Africa and Asia, although the converse is true in geographic terms. Again, the website contains the same content, but the map is animated, allowing the reader to witness the transition from the world as it is, to a map of the world distorted according to scale of consumption.

Other magazines supply moving content alongside the print version through a cover mounted CD-ROM. *Creative Review*, for example, is a print magazine that carries features about the advertising industry. In order to properly demonstrate TV, cinema and radio commercials, it supplies a CD-ROM on its first page, which carries sound and moving graphics. Likewise, *Shots*, an advertising magazine, comes complete with video cassette attached to its front cover. The advantages of having a forum to convey moving images and sound do not only apply to print publications catering for the image-making industries, though. *GQ* magazine, for example, reviews films and music within the print magazine, and the reviews are accompanied by a photograph – a still from a movie, promo video or concert performance. Occasionally, however, the magazine gives away a CD-ROM with every copy, on which entire promo videos or concert recordings can be shown, accompanied by music.

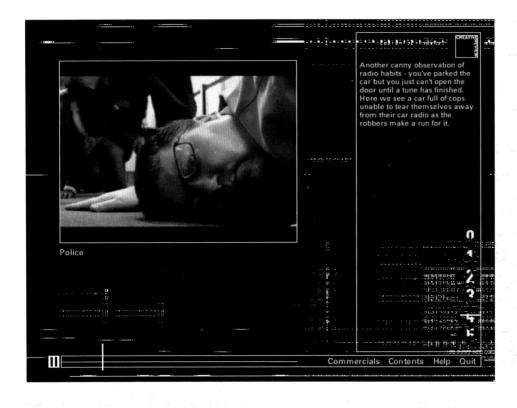

Another canny observation of radio habits - you've parked the car but you just can't open the door until a tune has finished. Here we see a car full of cops unable to tear themselves away from their car radio as the robbers make a run for it.

Police

Commercials Contents Help Quit

Colors
Issue: 25
Creative editor:
Adam Broomberg
Designer:
Runyon Hall
Italy

www.colors-
magazine.com
Issue: 25
Art director:
Fabrica
Italy

Creative Review
CD-ROM
UK

What does the future hold for magazines? One possibility is that over the course of the next few years, increasing numbers will go on-line, until the print magazine is threatened with extinction. On balance I think this is unlikely. Print has certain advantages over digital media: for a start, you can pick a magazine up to read on the train, and throw it away later, but a laptop is a permanent encumbrance. But beyond practicalities, readers enjoy print in a way that they don't enjoy digital media – reading a magazine is a tactile, sensuous experience. The smell of the ink, the feel of the paper in your hands, and the reassuring sense of substance suggested by the bulk of a publication are all peripheral, but important elements of the enjoyment experienced when reading a print magazine. It is also true, however, that readers also enjoy digital media in a way that they don't enjoy print: it is constantly updated, moving graphics and sound can be incorporated, and dialogues can be established, allowing the reader to truly become part of the magazines they loyally subscribe to.

As was described in the last chapter, many established print magazines are currently developing an on-line presence, whether it be a simple subscription information page or a fully-functional, semi-autonomous webzine. Today, we are beginning to see the launch of publications simultaneously in print and on the web. *Spoon*, a French fashion magazine, is a case in point. The contents page of the print version describes it as 'an electronic magazine created on the web', but in fact each issue is published simultaneously in print and on the web, and cross-references are continuously made between the two.

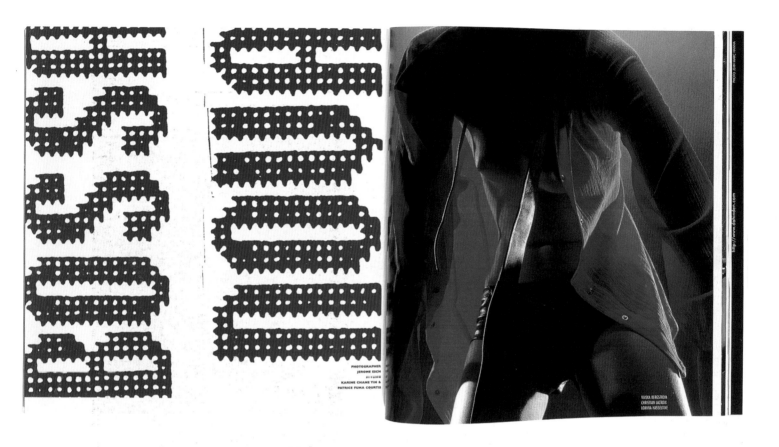

PHOTOGRAPHER
JEROME ESCH
STYLING
KARINE CHANE YIN &
PATRICE FUMA COURTIS

VIVEKA BERGSTROM
CHRISTIAN LACROIX
LOANNA HASSELTINE

http://www.dbhirden.com

PHOTO JEAN MARC HANIN

But will there still be a market for print magazines without a digital counterpart? The answer is yes, for a number of reasons: first, print is still convenient – it is a physical record that can be easily archived and referenced – a collection which seems, at least, more permanent than pages of a webzine, downloaded and filed in a digital storage system. Furthermore, as *Wired* magazine's Kevin Kelly has observed, as more and more of our world becomes digital, networked, automated or virtual, some of the activities or skills we take for granted today will come to be recognised as crafts, with comparatively few practitioners; by extension, their products, whether it be hand-made furniture, or printed magazines, will undergo a rise in desirability: they will become increasingly rare, and consequently valuable, in a world where plenitude is reducing costs and prices in other areas.

Some of the magazines featured in this book – *Visionaire*, *Shift!*, *Spirale* and *Form & Zweck*, for example – are already highly prized collectors' items, partly thanks to their uniqueness and rarity (the complexity of the production process in each case necessitates limited editions). It is likely that magazines such as these will provide a model on which increasing numbers of future magazines will be based. While print cannot hope to compete with digital media on the grounds of interactivity, for example, readers will increasingly take pleasure in their magazines as interesting physical objects.

As is noted at the beginning of this book, magazines over the course of history have had an unerring knack not only of adapting to suit the times in which they are produced, but in acting as the clearest mirror of that time, the most vivid historical snapshot. As long as they are willing and able to innovate and evolve, it seems sure that the magazine designers of today and tomorrow will continue to shape and reflect the times in which they live long into the next millennium.

Spoon
Issue: 4
Art directors:
Karine Chane Yin and
Patrice Fuma Courtis
France

www.spoon-
magazine.com
Issue: 4

Black + White
Issue: Feb 1999
Art director:
Marcelo Grand
Australia

Visionaire
Issue: 27 'Movement'
Art director:
Stephen Gan
USA

Form & Zweck
Issue: 15. 1999
Art director:
Gaston Isoz
Germany

Shift!
'Ahead of time'
Art director:
Anja Lutz
Germany

Contact details

Ampersand
+44 20 7 840 1111

Arena
+44 20 7 689 9999

Arena Homme Plus
+44 20 7 689 9999

Azure
+1 415 588 2588

Baseline
+44 1732 875 200

Bibel
+46 8 458 0150

Big
+1 212 343 3911

Billboard
+1 212 764 7300

Black and White
+61 2 9360 1422

Blue (Australia)
+61 2 9360 1422

Blue (US)
+1 212 777 0024

Blueprint
+44 20 7 706 4596

Colors
+39 422 6161

Common Ground
+1 415 459 4900

Crash
+33 1 43 45 74 61

Creative Review
+44 20 7 970 6276

Dazed & Confused
+44 20 7 336 0766

Design
+44 20 7 420 5200

dFusion
+44 20 8 255 2903

Domus
+39 2 824 721

Dutch
+31 71 516 15 30

The Editor
+44 20 7 278 2332

Elle
+44 20 7 208 3468

Emigré
+1 916 451 4344

ES
+44 20 7 938 6727

Esquire
+44 20 7 439 5000

Esterson Lackersteen
+44 20 7 684 6500

Eye
+44 20 8 565 4200

F100
+45 33 12 19 12

Flaunt
+1 323 650 9051

Form
+49 69 9433 0962

Form & Zweck
+49 30 655 5722

Frieze
+44 20 7 379 1533

Frost Design
+44 20 7 490 7994

The Guardian Weekend
+44 20 7 278 2332

Gear
+1 212 771 7000

GQ
+44 20 7 499 9080

Grafica
+34 93 31 51 819

Graphics International
+44 20 7 482 6011

I.D.
+1 212 447 1400

i-D
+44 20 7 813 6170

Immerse
+44 20 7 833 5626

The Interactive Bureau
+1 415 732 6123

Life
+1 212 685 7796

Loaded
+44 20 7 261 5562

Madison
+1 212 957 0017

Matador
+34 91 360 13 20

Nest
nestmag@aol.com

Nikkei Design
+813 5210 8311

Observer Life
+44 20 7 278 2332

Octavo
+44 20 7 403 4885

Pentagram
+44 20 7 229 3477

Private Eye
+44 20 7 437 4017

Ray Gun
+1 310 828 0522

RSA Journal
+44 20 7 839 7388

Shift!
+49 30 693 7814

Sight and Sound
+44 20 7 957 8916

sleazenation
+44 20 7 609 7757

The Spectator
+44 20 7 405 1706

Spoon
+33 1 46 03 67 68

Struktur Design
+44 20 7 833 5626

The Sunday Times
Magazine
+44 20 7 782 5000

Tank
+44 20 7 916 5264

Time
+1 212 522 1212

TypoGraphic
+44 20 1206 718 168

Typographische
Monatsblätter
+41 1 361 6795

Vanidad
+34 9 14 48 37 11

View on Colour
+33 1 44 31 77 91

Visionaire
+1 212 274 8959

Vogue
+44 20 7 499 9080

Vogue (France)
+33 1 53 711 014

Vogue (Italy)
+39 063 211657

Wallpaper
+44 20 7 322 1177

Wired
+1 415 276 5000

World Architecture
+44 20 7 560 4000

The World of Interiors
+44 20 7 499 9080

Further reading

The following list of titles is by no means definitive. Hundreds, if not thousands of books have been written that in some way discuss editorial design or designers. But the books below together make a fairly representative sample of the best in magazine design over the last half century.

33rd Publication Design Annual
Society of Publication Designers
Rockport Publishing, 1999
The US-based Society of Publication Designers' selection of the best current editorial work.

Brodovitch
Andy Grundberg
Thames and Hudson, 1999
Alexy Brodovitch (1898–1971), was best known for his work on *Harper's Bazaar*, and was extremely influential on the development of magazine design, not least for his use of the double page spread.

Cipe Pineles: a Life of Design
Martha Scotford
WW Nortin & Company, 1999
A scholarly look at the life and work of Cipe Pineles, who art directed, among others, *Glamour*, *Seventeen*, *Madmoiselle* and *Charm* magazines.

Covering the 60s:
George Lois, the Esquire Era
George Lois
Monacelli Press, 1996
A look at one of the classics from what some still see as the golden age of magazine publishing.

Covers and Jackets! What the Best Dressed
Books and Magazines are Wearing
Steven Heller and Anne Fink
Pbc Intl., 1993

Design Without Boundaries:
Visual Communication in Transition
Rick Poynor
Booth-Clibborn Editions, 1998
This collection of Poynor's journalism includes several critical essays on some of the most significant editorial design and designers of our times.

Great Magazine Covers of the World
Patricia Frantz Kery
Abbeville Press, 1982
A collection of hundreds of magazine covers, dating back over a century.

Inside Out: The Best of
National Geographic Diagrams
National Geographic Society, 1998
Despite its reputation for wildlife photography, there are some images even the *National Geographic*'s photographers couldn't get. Instead, its art directors commissioned these illustrations.

Magazine Editorial Graphics
Kaoru Yamashita
Nippan, 1997

Magazines: Inside and Out
Steven Heller and Teresa Fernandes
Pbc Intl, 1996

Nova
David Hillman, Harri Peccinotti
and David Gibbs
Pavillion Books, 1993

Magazine Design
Ruari McLean
Oxford University Press, 1969 (Out of print)
McLean's anthology contains many of the most notable examles of 1960s, editorial design, from the famous names – *Town*, *Queen*, *Twen* – to long-dead trade magazines.

The End of Print:
The Graphic Design of David Carson
Lewis Blackwell
Laurence King Publishing, 1995
An inquiry into the influential work of David Carson, designer of *Ray Gun* and *Beach Culture*, among others.

The Graphic Language of Neville Brody
Jon Wozencroft
Thames & Hudson, 1988
A look at the work of editorial pioneer Neville Brody, whose work on *The Face* impacted profoundly on the look of magazines in the 1980s.

Tibor Kalman
ed: Peter Hall
Booth-Clibborn Editions, 1998
An overview of the career of the multi-faceted Tibor Kalman, whose editorial credits include *Art Forum*, *Interview* and *Colors* magazines.

Web Sites That Work
Roger Black with Sean Elder
Adobe Press, 1997
The well-known magazine designer discusses his views on design and communication in relation to the web.

Credits/acknowledgements

Many thanks to all who provided advice and information for this book - and especially to Chris Barrett, Tim Fendley, Robin Richmond and Ben Tappenden. Another thank you to those who supplied material or consented to be interviewed. Thanks too to my editor at RotoVision, Angie Patchell, and Xavier Young for the magazine photography.

A final thank you also goes to Struktur Design, for advice, insight and a fine job on the layout.

NATIONAL GEOGRAPHIC FEBRUARY 1997 THE DAWN OF HUMANS KHANS ARMIES

A R E N A APRIL 1999/ISSUE 97 open 24 hours 10/98

COLORS 25 FAT·GRASSO Who's that girl?

cover magazine April 1999 Issue No 19

W I R E D 7.01 W W W I E C M

VOL 4 SUMMER OF LOVE SP001

DBK issue 39

sleazenation NOVEMBER 1998 VOLUME 2 ISSUE 10

A R E N A JANUARY/FEBRUARY 1999/ISSUE 85 gear THE MODEL ISSUE INSIDE THE YAKUZA SHANE MOSLEY GRIZZLY OBSESSION SLICK RICK DEAD ROCK STARS

- LES PUBLICATIONS CONDÉ NAST S.A. - FALL & W 1995 - N° 758 - DM 30 - FS 720 - ATS 100 - LIR 30.000 - 7512

CASH FOR CLICKS - DISCOVER THE POWER OF HOW TO SPEND YOUR RICH SITE BUSINESS

DESIGN 479 NOVEMBER 1988 GRAPHICS

QUARTERLY MAGAZINE +10 | SPRING 1997

APRIL 1999 VOGUE CONDÉ NAST PUBLICATION

GQ MARCH 1999 Cool, slightly enigmatic, perfectly poised (p142)

COLORS 8: RELIGION September 1994 ☼ Bhadrapad 2051 ☾ Jamada Al-Thani 1415 ☗ Sharivar 1363 AY ✡ Elul 5754 ☪ Asmà 151 † September 1994 COLORS 8: RELIGION DEATH MORTE

COLORS 24

COLORS 23 GIFTS FOR THE FAMILY REGALI PER LA FAMIGLIA

January 1996

FALL/WINTER 1991 1991 1/N. 1 1/N.1 VOL. UNITED COLORS OF BENETTON

COLORS una revista sobre el resto del mundo (It's a baby!) (es un bebé!) VOL. 1/N. 1 1991

COSMOPOLITAN February 1999

COLORS

QUARTERLY MAGAZINE #17 | SUMMER 97 | $7.50 £ FS 349

)transfert 1002 Gueules d'avenir · Haut-Brion high-tech · Ramoji

frieze

ISSUE 45 MARCH · APRIL 1999

COLORS 8: RELIGION September 1994 ☼ Bhadrapad 2051 ☾ Jamada Al-Thani 1415 ☗ Sharivar 1363 AY ✡ Elul 5754 ☪ Asmà 151 † Septembre 1994 COLORS 8: RELIGION

COLORS ◷ TIME ZEIT DESIGNERS IN LA ILLUSTRATION BROWSERS THAT THINK ADRIAN FRUTIGER

ICON VAL KILMER GENERAL ALEKSANDR LEBED CLIVE DAVIS FEBRUARY 1999

domus 787 Novembre November 1996 ARRIBAS, ETOY, GEHRY, GIOVANNONI, ISOZAKI, PESCE, STERN, VENTURI/SCOTT BROWN, VON MOOS, WILSON

DAZED&CONFUSED #51 KATE MOSS ISAAC HAYES JOHN WATERS SAUL WILLIAMS NUDIE COHN CAMERON JAMIE BEN LEE

JUNE 1999 ELLE THE WORLD'S BIGGEST-SELLING FASHION MAGAZINE FRANCE FF36.00 US $4.95 BELGIUM BF213 ITALY LIO...

DAZED&CONFUSED #34 DAMIEN HIRST JAKE & DINOS CHAPMAN FASHION BRITISH ART SUPPLEMENT RAY WINSTONE MIKE MYERS PHOTEK

i-D MAGAZINE JANUARY/FEBRUARY 1999 THE EMERGENCY ISSUE NO. 183

Esquire MY BUNNY VALENTINE FEBRUARY 1999 VOLUME 8 NUMBER 2 02/03

GQ MAY 1999 'Playing Apocalypse Now with the cast of Deliverance' (p100)

Big Music+Fashion Number 20 UK £ 7.95 España Pts. 1.200

wallpaper* march 1999 domestic boom | köln report | on board airbus | coffee tables | los angeles luxe | perfect date | steam cuisine | fukuoka city | antumalal lodge | après chic Australia $ 8.50 Belgium FL ... Canada $ 8.50 France FF 45 Germany DM 20 Holland HFl 12.50 Italy Lire ... Spain PTS ... Sweden SKr ...

Vol. CXIII. No. 1

35 black+white aleksandra vujcic opell ross sante d'orazio pj harvey

blue the new ADVENTURE LIFESTYLE december 1998

MATADOR 1998 G H

MATADOR 1996 B